Philosophy of Mind: A Very Short Introduction

VERY SHORT INTRODUCTIONS are for anyone wanting a stimulating and accessible way into a new subject. They are written by experts, and have been translated into more than 45 different languages.

The series began in 1995, and now covers a wide variety of topics in every discipline. The VSI library currently contains over 700 volumes—a Very Short Introduction to everything from Psychology and Philosophy of Science to American History and Relativity—and continues to grow in every subject area.

Very Short Introductions available now:

For more information visit our website

www.oup.com/vsi/

Barbara Gail Montero

PHILOSOPHY OF MIND

A Very Short Introduction

OXFORD
UNIVERSITY PRESS

OXFORD
UNIVERSITY PRESS

Great Clarendon Street, Oxford, OX2 6DP,
United Kingdom

Oxford University Press is a department of the University of Oxford.
It furthers the University's objective of excellence in research, scholarship,
and education by publishing worldwide. Oxford is a registered trade mark of
Oxford University Press in the UK and in certain other countries

First Edition published 2022

Impression: 1

Published in the United States of America by Oxford University Press
198 Madison Avenue, New York, NY 10016, United States of America

British Library Cataloguing in Publication Data
Data available

Library of Congress Control Number: 2021942656

ISBN 978-0-19-880907-4

Printed in Great Britain by
Ashford Colour Press Ltd, Gosport, Hampshire

Contents

Preface

When you step on a tack in bare feet, pain receptors at the site of the injury send electrical signals via nerve fibres to your spinal cord and ultimately to your brain where they pass into areas responsible for physical sensation, thought, and emotion. The result is that unpleasant feeling we call pain. Now imagine that the details of this neurophysiological explanation of pain are filled in. Would we have a complete account of your feeling of pain? If pain is nothing more than a neurophysiological process, we would. Yet if that's all there is to it, why is the pain of stepping on a tack exclusively in your foot, whereas the neurophysiology of pain implicates peripheral nerves, spinal cord, brain stem and cerebrum?

Granny Smith apples look green to me. And if you have normal colour vision, they look green to you too. Or at least, both you and I will describe Granny Smith apples as green. But how do I know that you experience their colour the way I do? How do I know that your experience of what I call 'green' isn't exactly like what I experience when I see red? It seems that while I can hear your words and see your actions, only you can know what you are experiencing in your own mind; only you can know what it is like for you to see Granny-Smith-green. Can we prove that your experience of green is the same as mine by observing our brains? Let's say that when you see green, your brain is in the exact same configuration as mine is when I see green. Would this show that you and I are having the same kind of experiences? Or would the possibility remain that our brains could behave exactly alike while our individual experiences differ?

If you play chess, you've most likely lost a game to a computer. Although high-level chess skill was once thought of as an exclusively human ability, computers now excel at the game. Does this mean that computers think? And if so, do they think essentially in the same way we do? Or is there something about information processing in a biological brain that precludes replication in an electronic brain? Perhaps computers ponder chess moves, diagnose diseases, and analyse stock trades, but could a computer ever experience joy or feel sad? Could a computer ever be conscious? While humans are composed almost entirely of oxygen, carbon, hydrogen, nitrogen, calcium, and phosphorus, computer chips are primarily silicon. Does this difference in elemental makeup matter when it comes to deciding whether minds can emerge from computer chips?

These are some of the puzzles that anchor philosophy of mind, a field of study with both cross-cultural roots and cross-disciplinary connections that investigates thoughts, emotions, desires, beliefs, pains, pleasures, perceptions, and consciousness.

Many questions that philosophers of mind address overlap with questions scientists investigate. Philosophers want to understand the nature of consciousness; neuroscientists and psychologists do too. Philosophers want to decipher the relationship between language and thought; linguists do as well. Philosophers study rational decision-making, as do economists, and attempt to discern the ultimate constituents of reality, which is also the domain of physics. Yet, despite being one of the branches of the interdisciplinary study of the mind called 'cognitive science', philosophy of mind is typically not considered science.

To a large extent, philosophy and science employ different methods. Scientists conduct experiments or systematically collect measurable data and develop theories or models based on what they have found, while philosophers tend to rely on 'armchair', or 'a priori', enquiry, which means they like to think (in or out of an armchair) about what makes sense. Philosophers also tend to cherish the history and heroes of their discipline more than scientists do. When philosophers want to understand the nature of causation, they may delve into Aristotle's view of the four different kinds of causation—material, formal, efficient, and final—while a scientist might win a Nobel Prize for research on the nature of light without even having heard of Ptolemy's law of refraction.

And yet, these divisions are not absolute. Some philosophers cut their ties to history, eschew the armchair approach, and instead conduct experiments, systematically collect data, and base their theories on their findings. Furthermore, scientists can be history buffs, and they frequently engage in a priori reasoning: could there be confounding factors in an experiment? What are the possible explanations of the data? Which of two equally empirically supported theories is more likely true? Answering such questions can be done comfortably from an armchair.

There is a lively debate among philosophers today about the usefulness of empirical results in philosophical investigations of the mind. One side of the debate sees empirical work as the only means of progress, while the other side views philosophy of mind as belonging to the branch of philosophy called 'metaphysics', a branch of philosophy that aims to uncover truths about the world that hold necessarily, truths that would hold even if the scientific laws as we know them were different. As these metaphysicians (as they are called) see it, the questions they investigate are beyond the scope of science since they are questions not about our world but about hypothetical worlds, worlds that may contain nothing other than two black spheres, each the mirror image of the other, or miles upon miles of fake barns, or inhabitants carrying little boxes that house what they call a 'beetle'.

As novelists need not conduct real-world experiments to test whether their plots could be realized, philosophical thought experiments may seem rather more like literature than science. Furthermore, great works of literature frequently probe the perennial questions of philosophy. For example, in struggling to understand the world from others' perspectives, the central character in Marcel Proust's seven-volume work *In Search of Lost Time* seems well aware of what philosophers have referred to as the 'epistemic gap' between what science can reveal about a person and what we know about being a person from our own case. And Mary Shelley's *Frankenstein*—a novel written while she was pregnant and perhaps contemplating the fear, awe, and enormous godlike power of birth—grapples with, among other philosophical matters, our moral obligations to complex, conscious beings who differ from us.

Still, even though the best thought experiments may have a literary element, philosophy—apart from such gems as Nietzsche's *Thus Spoke Zarathustra* and Kierkegaard's *Either/ Or*—is no more literature than it is science. The conclusions drawn from thought experiments in philosophy of mind are much more explicit than those found in fiction. Subtlety in literature is a virtue, whereas the arguments in philosophy of mind, rather fittingly, typically aim to hit you over the head. Besides, scientists, too, conduct thought experiments: Newton never fired a cannon from the top of an extremely tall mountain; Galileo probably never dropped anything off the leaning tower of Pisa; and Schrödinger didn't even own a cat. What, then, is a distinctly philosophical approach to studying the mind? We shall return to this question, though, as you will see, like most questions we shall grapple with, it will ultimately be left unresolved. Indeed, the aim of philosophy—and, here, perhaps more so than other disciplines—is not so much to find answers to questions but to formulate the questions themselves.

Acknowledgements

The French mathematician and philosopher Blaise Pascal commented in a 1657 letter that he would have written less, had he had time to do so. I thank Oxford University Press for their patience. I would also like to thank my City University of New York graduate and undergraduate students who commented on drafts of the book, the friends, colleagues, and quite a few strangers who responded over email to my urgent requests for advice, and, most of all, Rajkumar Nanavati who read the entire manuscript twice and offered invaluable suggestions.

Acknowledgements

List of illustrations

Chapter 1
Dualism

Dualism in philosophy of mind is the theory that the mind is distinct from the body; it is the theory that a human being comprises not only a physical body, generally encompasing torso, limbs, head, and neck, but also an immaterial mind, which is seen as the seat of thought and conscious experience; it is the theory that philosophy of mind cut its teeth on, and, though widely criticized, it continues to command the attention of contemporary philosophers who puzzle over thought experiments that seem to suggest the theory is true.

The Mary thought experiment

Imagine Mary, a brilliant neuroscientist who has spent her entire life in an environment devoid of colour. Her walls, furniture, and lab equipment are shades of grey; if her knife slips while slicing steel-grey tomatoes, she bleeds out ebony blood; she even dreams in black and white. However, convinced that the grass is indeed greener than the grey stuff she's familiar with, she devotes herself to figuring out what it is like to see colour. Through black and white books and computer monitors, she learns about the surface reflectance properties of objects, the wavelengths of light, the neurophysiology of colour vision; she reads poetry about colour— 'the Red—Blaze—is the Morning— | The Violet—is Noon—'; she studies the moods that colours are thought to signify in various cultures. Eventually, Mary learns everything about the experience of seeing colour that can be taught in black and white. Is there anything left for Mary to be curious about? It seems that there is, since if she were to leave her black and white environment, she'd be surprised: 'So that's what green looks like! Now I know!' Yet if she learns something new upon encountering colours, what she learns cannot be a physical fact about colour vision, since she had mastered all of these in the lab. Thus, the knowledge she gains upon seeing colours must concern the workings of the immaterial mind.

This thought experiment is a variation on the contemporary Australian philosopher Frank Jackson's 'knowledge argument', so called because its starting premise establishes what Mary knows: everything about colour that can be conveyed in a black and white environment. As proponents of the knowledge argument see it, this premise, combined with the premise that Mary is surprised at seeing colour for the first time, implies that inside her lab, she didn't have complete knowledge of colour vision. She knew all the physical facts, but she didn't understand the non-physical aspects of experiencing color. Thus, they conclude that dualism, which is the view that the mind is not physical and, as such, is of a different nature from the body, is true.

How convincing is the knowledge argument? Could it be that Mary wouldn't be surprised upon leaving her achromatic environment? Due to technological advancements in optics, partially colour-blind individuals can now don colour-enhancing glasses and see what they've missed. And some media reports indicate that the experience is so moving, so startling, so wondrous that these green gazing greenhorns are sometimes brought to tears, which suggests that Mary would at least learn something new by the experience. Then again, these partially colour-blind individuals who are brought to tears didn't have the type of extensive scientific knowledge of colour that Mary possesses. And some philosophers think this matters, arguing that it is unfathomable what knowing *all* the physical facts of colour vision amounts to, and, thus, we cannot rule out the possibility that Mary, before she escapes, can know all there is to know about the experience of seeing colour.

Other critics of Jackson's argument think that even if Mary were to have a gap in her knowledge before she sees colour for the first time, this would only mean that there was something she didn't *know* about the world; it wouldn't mean that conscious experience is not a part of the physical world. What we know of the world is one thing; what the world is really like is something else. And still others claim that it is not possible to learn all the physical facts in a black and white environment. They claim that although Mary (from inside the lab) can't learn that seeing green is like *this*—where 'this' is filled in by that familiar experience you have when you see green—her experience of seeing green once she escapes is nonetheless physical.

Proponents of the knowledge argument aren't swayed. They contend that if the mind were physical, Mary would be able to learn everything about it in a black and white environment; for isn't one able to learn all the other physical aspects of colour vision without seeing colour? And as for the objection that we can't conceive of what it would be like to learn all the physical facts, they argue that even though there are a vast number of physical facts that Mary would need to learn, and even though we don't know today what all those facts are, we understand well enough what it would be like for her to learn further physical facts and that doing so would not enlighten her. Thus, they maintain, the gap in Mary's knowledge of the world implies that there is a gap in the physical world where the conscious experience of seeing green should be.

The mind–body problem

Philosophers who uphold dualism see it as a solution to one of the great problems in philosophy: the mind–body problem, which is the problem of specifying the relationship between the mind and the body. Is the mind distinct from the body and capable of existing on its own without any bodily substrate? Or is the mind a component of the brain, ceasing to exist upon bodily death? Dualists traditionally embrace the first option. They solve the mind–body problem—or, as it's sometimes put, the problem of explaining how the mind fits into the physical world—by specifying a clean break between mind and body. For the dualist, the mind, in contrast to all other bodily or physical things of this world—rocks, trees, tables, chairs—is an immaterial entity.

What makes the mind–body problem challenging is that there are reasons both to view the mind as a material part of our bodies and to view it as something immaterial. Think about the body from a biological perspective. Biology depicts human beings as aggregations of 37.2 trillion cells working together to form the tissues and organs that keep us ticking. And although there is much more to learn, it is natural to think that future discoveries will not reveal that in addition to being composed of cells, human beings house immaterial minds, minds that can't be understood in terms of cellular functions. The mind, from a biological perspective, is nothing more than the working brain, or, more specifically, in contrast to the parts of the brain that control digestion, respiration, and other autonomic processes, it is nothing other than the parts of the working brain that beget thinking, feeling, emoting, and the like.

Now consider the workings of your own mind from a first-person point of view. Are you in pain? What are you seeing? What thoughts are going through your head? Without consulting an fMRI scan, without consulting the experts, without even turning to Google, you can answer these questions. To be sure, a friend may understand better than you do that you are envious of and not actually angry at your colleague who is making twice your salary. Still, even if we are sometimes mistaken about what goes on in our minds, we nonetheless seem able to introspect, more or less accurately, our mental lives. And what we learn about our minds through introspection doesn't seem to apply to our brains. From an fMRI scan, scientists might be able to *infer* that you are feeling cheerful, but introspection apparently requires no inferences; introspection might occasionally mislead, but when it works, it seems to put you in direct contact with your mind. And introspection, although it may reveal that you are thinking about the number eight, can't reveal (directly) that there is activity in your bilateral intraparietal sulci. If we can introspect our minds but not our brains, the mind, it would seem, is not a component of the brain.

We also tend to think that everything that happens is ultimately constrained by either the probabilistic or deterministic laws of physics but also that at least some of our choices—Chocolate or vanilla? Train or bus? Tango or Cha-cha-cha?—are not constrained in this way. In other words, it seems both that the mind is a material thing governed by the laws of physics and also that, regardless of which way the physical particles are pointing, you and your partner are free to choose to tango.

Could the mind be both an aspect of the functioning body and something separate from our bodies, both material and immaterial, both entirely explicable by science and something that science can never fully illuminate? In everyday life, we frequently maintain contradictory beliefs; in the poet Walt Whitman's words, we 'contain multitudes'. Yet for philosophers, contradictions are generally like nails on a chalkboard and, thus, in studying the mind, they are driven to figure out where our thinking about mind and body has gone wrong.

Dualism in ancient times

One sometimes hears that a certain philosophical theory is as old as philosophy itself. Dualism, however, is older. As a philosophical theory, it goes back at least to Plato, who, writing in Greece in the 4th century BCE, saw human beings as composed of a material body and an immaterial mind, or what he thought of as a body and a soul. (Philosophers frequently use the terms 'immaterial mind' and 'soul' interchangeably.) Plato's dualism is well captured in his dialogue the *Phaedo*, in which Socrates describes death as being the point at which the soul separates from the body: 'Death is this,' Socrates tells us, 'the body having come to be apart from, separated from the soul, alone by itself, and the soul's being apart, alone by itself, separated from the body.' Socrates is propounding not only dualism of mind and body, according to which human beings have two components, but also the view that, although mind and body are yoked during our earthly lives, these two components come apart upon death, the body to turn to dust and the soul to flourish in the afterlife.

Dualism's history can also be traced through religious texts. The Buddhist text, the *Visuddhimagga*, written in the 5th century CE in Sri Lanka, presents a version of dualism in which the soul and body are interdependent. According to this text, mind and body are analogous to a blind person and a non-ambulatory person who is being carried on the blind person's back: one serves as the other's legs and the other serves as the one's eyes. Just as the blind individual and the individual being carried need each other's assistance, the mind requires the body to exist and the body cannot function without the mind. This Buddhist conception of the mind does not come with the extra perk of immortality, for if mind and body are mutually dependent, then one can't survive without the other. Nonetheless, it is a form of dualism since it posits that mind and body are distinct entities.

Many religious traditions, however, do uphold dualism with the extra perk. For example, immortality is the central concern in what has come to be known as the *Egyptian Book of the Dead*, an ancient funerary text, which was in widespread use about a

1. Archaeological remains of a Neanderthal infant burial, possibly adorned with red deer maxilla, from the Amud paleoanthropological site in Israel.

thousand years before Plato wrote of Socrates, and which can be understood as the soul's travel guide to the afterlife. There is even some indication that the Neanderthals may have had a dualistic understanding of mind and body: archaeological data reveals that Neanderthals had ritualistic burial practices, burying deceased group members with care and occasionally adorning their graves with animal bones or, possibly, flowers (Figure 1).

We can only speculate as to why they did this. But it could be that they believed that the soul was separate from the body and need not perish with it.

Immortality of the soul, from antiquity up to today, is a precept also of Christianity, Islam, Hinduism, Judaism (at least, arguably), and many other religions.

What is philosophically interesting about dualism's long lineage is not necessarily the arguments that were given for it, as sometimes there weren't any—or at least not any that today's philosophers would call 'arguments'. Rather, what is philosophically significant is the mere fact that it does have this lineage. The 20th-century Austrian-British philosopher Ludwig Wittgenstein held that philosophy is iatrogenic: it aims merely to cure illnesses that it itself has created, merely 'to show the fly the way out of the fly-bottle'. Some philosophy may be iatrogenic, but one side of the mind-body conundrum—our inclination to think of the mind as distinct from the body—arose even before the discipline of philosophy existed.

Cartesian dualism

Although *The Book of the Dead* may have been an ancient Egyptian best-seller, the central texts in contemporary philosophy of mind pass over the question of immortality. Instead, contemporary philosophers focus on the question of whether it is possible—possible, that is, in the abstract sense in which a flying elephant is possible were you to change the laws of physics and evolutionary biology—for the mind and body to be distinct. This approach to the mind–body problem—looking to prove that the mind is distinct from the body (regardless of whether it survives bodily death)—has its roots in the 17th-century works of the French mathematician and philosopher René Descartes, who is seen, as the founder of modern philosophy. While contemporary philosophy is sometimes described as a series of footnotes to Plato, contemporary philosophy of mind might be better described as a footnote to Descartes.

Before Descartes, nature was understood much as Aristotle envisioned it: suffused with mind, with purpose and intention and other psychological attributes that were impenetrable to quantitative analysis. If you wanted to understand why acorns fall, you had to investigate the acorns' desires and perhaps even hopes to arrive at their natural resting place, which for anything with mass was the centre of the earth. Paving the way for the scientific revolution, Descartes siphoned off the lusts and longings from matter, leaving behind a material world of mountains, molecules, and human bodies that was amenable to quantitative analysis, a world of unthinking, unfeeling, spatially extended things, a world, as Descartes put it, whose essence is extension in length, breadth, and depth. In contrast, the mental world—the world of thoughts, beliefs, desires, and sensory experiences—has no extension. But although siphoning off the mental from the material opened the material world to modern science, it simultaneously isolated the mental world from scientific scrutiny.

Descartes upheld a form of dualism that has come to be known as 'Cartesian dualism', or 'interactive dualism', according to which mind and body are distinct (that's the dualism part) yet causally interact with each other (that's the interactive part). That there are causal interactions between mind and body is, according to Descartes, common sense: your thought that you are thirsty (which is something going on in your mind) may cause you to pick up a glass of water (which is an action of your body); your (bodily) sprained ankle may cause you to feel pain (which is a process in your mind).

Why think that dualism is true? Descartes argues as follows: mind and body can't be one and the same thing since something whose sole nature is extension (the body) could exist without the mind, and something whose sole nature is thought (the mind) could exist without the body. Thus, mind and body, he concludes, must be distinct; 'my mind', as Descartes puts it, 'is entirely and truly distinct from my body, and may exist without it'. In other words, Descartes argues that because it is *possible* for mind and body to exist on their own, mind and body *actually are* distinct.

It might seem a leap to go from statements about what could be the case (that mind could exist without body and vice versa) to what actually is the case (that mind and body are distinct). And it is true that in philosophy courses, Descartes's argument for the 'real distinction' between mind and body is frequently presented as a paragon of the almost miraculous power of philosophical argumentation, power that permits one to draw conclusions about what is actually the case from premises about what is merely possible. But the move is not miraculous at all: as Descartes understands it, for one thing to be truly distinct from another thing just is for that one thing to possibly exist without the other. Thus, far from a leap, Descartes's conclusion about the actual distinction between mind and body follows, by definition, from their possible distinction.

The question of how he arrives at this possibility, however, is another matter. Descartes presents his argument for dualism in the *Meditations*, a book which he dedicated to the sacred Faculty of Theology of the University of Paris. He wanted the Faculty to officially approve of the book so he could avoid legal trouble. Whether this was his sole motivation for arguing for dualism is unknown, as is whether he was ever granted the Faculty's official approval. What is known is that the book sparked a vibrant debate. Princess Elisabeth of Bohemia, in her correspondence with Descartes, identifies what is now generally seen as its fatal flaw. Elisabeth asks, 'How can an unextended thing push the body to engage in actions?' Causation, Elisabeth points out (and as was generally accepted at the time), requires contact—it requires one thing to touch another, much as one billiard ball causes another to move—yet something unextended can never come into contact with something extended. Thus, with respect to the unextended mind and extended body, never the twain shall meet. Although Descartes assumes that a desire to drink water, for example, could cause a body to pick up a glass of water, given the conception of causation Descartes was working with, mind–body causation was impossible. It is easier to imagine the mind as material, Elisabeth told Descartes, than it is to imagine causal relations between an immaterial mind and a material body.

Philosophers in the latter part of the 17th century and beginning of the 18th century offered rather creative solutions to the problem of mind–body causation. Some adopted a theory of mind according to which mind and body never causally interact but run along parallel tracks. The German polymath Gottfried Leibniz upheld such a 'parallelism', or what was referred to as 'pre-established harmony'. He likened mind and body to two synchronized clocks: just as both clocks will strike three at the same time, even though one is not causing the other to chime, so too your arm will reach towards a glass of water when you desire a drink because mind and body are synchronized, even though your desire does not cause you to do so. What explains such synchronicity? On Leibniz's account, mind and body were wound up, or 'pre-established', at the outset by God.

Others addressed the problem Elisabeth posed for Cartesian dualism by eliminating the material side of the equation and advocating 'idealism', a theory according to which the entire material world is merely a construct of the mind. According to the best-known proponent of idealism, the early 18th-century Irish philosopher George Berkeley, pain follows bodily damage not because bodily damage causes pain, but because this is the logical progression of ideas in the mind of God.

Leibniz and Berkeley may have avoided the problem of mind–body causation, yet most philosophers today would say that they did so at an exorbitant cost. Not only were their ontological conceptions of reality outré, but they also made God do some heavy lifting to make it appear to humankind as if mind–body causation occurs. Besides, today's dualists have another way around Elisabeth's objection. Newton's law of universal gravitation—a law that states that massive objects attract other massive objects in direct proportion to the product of their mass and in inverse proportion to the square of the distance between them—broached the possibility of causation without contact. Newton's law, for example, accounts for how the gravitational pull of the moon and sun on the earth, affects the rise and fall of ocean tides without bringing contact into the picture. To be

sure, Newton's law of gravity was eventually superseded, yet
Descartes's mechanistic picture of causation, according to which
causation requires one thing to physically bump into another,
never recovered. As the linguist and philosopher Noam Chomsky
puts it, Newton exorcized the Cartesian body but left the
Cartesian mind perfectly intact. Dualism may be open to
objections, but the difficulty Elisabeth posed for Descartes is no
longer one of them.

Why only two?

Are we made out of one kind of thing, namely, matter? Or are we
made up of two kinds of things, mind and matter? Although many
debates in philosophy revolve around these possibilities, there are
other options. For example, you could maintain, as Berkeley did,
that there is one kind of thing, but that it is not material. Or you
could maintain that there are two kinds of things but that they are
both material, which would be the case, for example, if the world
were to exclusively comprise ordinary matter and dark matter
(assuming that dark matter is fundamentally different from
ordinary matter). Finally, one can believe that there are more than
two kinds of things; matter, both dark and ordinary, may be on
this list as may be any number of things, including dark energy,
abstract numbers, and moral values. When counting over two,
philosophers tend to go with three or many, but the possibilities
are in principle endless.

Even Descartes, some argue, may not have been hung up on two.
Though he presents an argument for dualism in the *Meditations*,
he also says that sensations, such as hunger, thirst, and pain, arise
from the 'union and as it were intermingling of the mind with the
body'. Such comments motivate some to understand Descartes,
not as a dualist, but as a trialist, according to which human beings
are composed of mind stuff, bodily stuff, and a stuff that consists
of the union of mind and body.

A trialistic picture of the person is also a characteristic of Akan philosophy. Akan philosophy, which arose out of the oral tradition in West Africa (primarily Ghana), understands a person to comprise an *okra*, which is variously translated as 'soul' or 'life-force', a *honam*, which is generally translated as 'body', and a *sumsun*, sometimes translated as 'personality' or 'character'. One's soul, on the Akan conception, persists after one's bodily death, while one's personality, though not just a bodily feature of a person, is extinguished with one's last breath.

Counting the kinds of things that make up a person, however, is not straightforward. Indeed, it is not even obvious how to answer the question, 'how many kinds of things are in my fruit bowl?' Should I answer, 'one' since every item is a fruit? Or is it 'three' since I have apples, oranges, and a grapefruit? Or should I say 'two': citrus and pome? Should the air count? Dust? The answer depends on what matters to you. So what matters in counting up the kinds of things that a person comprises? The Ghanaian philosopher Kwame Gyekye, who died in 2019, argues that because the body is physical while neither the *okra* nor the *sumsun* is, the Akan person should be understood as comprising just two kinds of things, one of which is immaterial, the other material. Contemporary philosophers of mind generally focus on the divide between the material and the immaterial as well.

The zombie argument

Despite the popularity of the genre, it is not true that most pieces of writing are improved by the addition of zombies. *Pride and Prejudice and Zombies* is a fun read, but it's not better than the original. However, in the case of Descartes's argument for dualism, the zombified version is often seen as superior. The so-called 'zombie argument' has little to do with the sort of zombies that lumber gracelessly along dimly lit streets and murder honourable and often stunningly beautiful bystanders. Rather, the 'zombies' that inhabit philosophical thought experiments are intended to be understood as molecule-for-molecule duplicates of sentient human beings that are exactly like us save for the fact that they lack consciousness. They might scream when in pain, but they don't feel a thing. And their addition to Descartes's argument improves it by clarifying what is at stake.

Descartes argued that it is possible for his mind to exist without his body and for his body to exist without his mind; the zombie argument distils what is frequently thought of as Descartes's crucial step: the possibility of a fully functioning body existing without an accompanying mind.

Imagine a world—a 'zombie world'—that duplicates our world's fundamental physical particles and forces. This duplicate world would look exactly like ours; it would have oceans, mountains, valleys, and plains just like ours. Yet no one in it is conscious. Your zombie double would do everything you do and would have a brain that functions just like yours except they would have no inner life, no consciousness, no experiences of green or anything else. Could there be a zombie world? Contemporary dualists think so because they believe that imagination (more specifically, careful imagination or *conceivability*) serves as a guide to possibility, much in the way that your ability to clearly imagine the leftover soup fitting in a container would serve as a guide to the possibility of its fitting. Furthermore, they argue that because zombies are possible, consciousness must be something other than a physical aspect of the world; it must be an additional component of our world that does not necessarily arise out of the organization of the forces and particles of physics.

The prominence of zombies in philosophical debates about dualism is largely due to writings of the contemporary philosopher David Chalmers, who takes the zombie argument as a compelling reason to think that the mind is immaterial. Like Descartes's argument for dualism, the zombie argument turns on the idea that the possibility of a fully functioning body without a mind reveals that the mind is distinct from the body. Think about it this way. To grow a marigold, you need not only fertile soil, sun, and plenty of water, but also a marigold seed, because, after all, if you were to have the sun, soil, and water without the seed, nothing would sprout. As proponents of the zombie argument see it, the sun, soil, and water are analogous to the body, and the seed is analogous to the mind: the body alone does not suffice for a human being; body alone, as they see it, is a zombie. Thus, the possibility of zombies, it is thought, shows that the mind is something additional to the body that it adorns, something that had to be planted.

Questioning conceivability arguments

The zombie argument turns on three assumptions: (1) that we can imagine zombies, (2) that our ability to do so implies that such creatures are possible, and (3) that the possibility of zombies substantiates dualism—all of which can be questioned.

The inference from imaginability to possibility has come under the most attack. Both Descartes' argument and the zombie argument are referred to as 'conceivability arguments' because they draw conclusions about what is possible based on what we can clearly imagine, or conceive. Though some philosophers champion the move from conceivability to possibility, arguing that we often use imagination, or conceivability, as a guide to possibility—remember your leftover soup—others disparage it, arguing that before we know the relevant details of the domain of enquiry, what we can imagine about that domain is irrelevant to what is possible in it and, thus, our ability to conceive of zombies does not imply that these humourless creatures are possible. These critics may point out, for example, that before you learn the proof that there are infinitely many prime numbers, you might be able to imagine that the primes stop at some point, yet, it is not only true, but necessarily true that there are infinitely many primes; similarly, you might be able to imagine a finite staircase

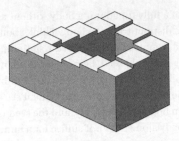

2. The Penrose stairs, also known as the 'impossible staircase', created independently by the Swedish graphic artist Oscar Reutersvärd in 1937 and later by the British mathematician Roger Penrose in collaboration with his father, the psychiatrist Lionel Penrose.

that ascends forever by mentally picturing the Penrose stairs (Figure 2). Yet a staircase that ascends forever is impossible. In tune with critics of the Mary thought experiment, critics of the zombie argument maintain that the world is, is one thing; what we imagine or *seem* to imagine is something else.

Defenders of conceivability arguments stress that in purported cases of imagining impossibilities, we are not *clearly* imagining an endless finite staircase or an end to the primes; to clearly conceive of the staircase is to apprehend it as finite; to clearly conceive of the prime number is to understand, among other things, Euclid's proof. In other words, defenders of conceivability arguments maintain that it is only after working out the relevant details that your imagination of an endless finite staircase, a terminus to the primes, or what have you becomes a reliable guide to what is possible in these domains.

But now, with these higher standards for conceivability, one might question whether we actually can conceive of zombies. Can we clearly imagine creatures that are physically, chemically, and biologically just like us but lacking consciousness? And what assurance is there that we have worked out all the relevant details of our conception of such creatures? The possibility of zombies,

16

Chalmers admits, does depend on 'brute intuition', but, as he sees it, this is no different from how the possibility of a mile-high unicycle depends on intuition: yes, it's merely my intuition that tells me that a mile-high unicycle is possible, yet, he argues, it's obvious that this intuition, just like the intuition that zombies are possible, is correct.

Moreover, according to dualists, common sense is on their side. We describe some people as, 'mentally fit, yet physically disabled', and others as having 'lost their minds despite having healthy bodies'. We talk of the mental side of sports—what you need to do to get that mental edge—which we think of as different from merely physical training. Indeed, the United States constitutional protection of free speech seems predicated on a dualism between mind and body: physical assault, which can damage the body, is prohibited under the constitution, while—unless it leads to or threatens bodily harm—verbal assault, which can damage the mind, is not. Thus, it seems that, somewhere deep in our psyches, a dualism of mind and body is inscribed.

And yet, not only do our mental inscriptions sometimes mislead us, but what is obviously true for one philosopher may be clearly false for another. Thus, the debate over the status of dualism goes on. In fact, it is difficult to imagine the discipline of philosophy of mind, as it is commonly practised, without it. The standard arguments for dualism, perhaps more than the arguments for any other central theories in philosophy of mind, rely on a priori premises, that is, premises which can be supported by mere thought—or, rather, I should say by hard, tireless thought. And a priori reasoning is what, traditionally, philosophy depends on. In this way, dualism not only heralded the start of traditional philosophy of mind, but its death may herald its end as well.

Chapter 2
Behaviourism

The mid-20th-century English philosopher Gilbert Ryle dubbed
Descartes's dualism of mind and body 'the dogma of the Ghost in
the machine'; Cartesian dualism, he opined, 'is not merely an
assemblage of particular mistakes' but is 'one big mistake'. Putting
his critique with 'deliberate abusiveness', Ryle aimed to topple not
just Descartes's theory of mind, but also the long chain of dualistic
thinkers that reached up to his day.

Objections to mind–body dualism had surfaced before. As we saw
in the previous chapter, Descartes was criticized by Princess
Elisabeth of Bohemia for being unable to account for mind–body
causation: given the 17th-century conception of causation as
requiring contact, it was very difficult, if not impossible, to
understand how an unextended mind could have a causal effect on
an extended body. Yet, while Elisabeth critiqued the details of
dualism, Ryle went for the jugular. His aim was to demolish the
entire theory, to obliterate what he saw as a philosopher's myth.

The category mistake

Descartes's big mistake, according to Ryle, was thinking of mind
and body as distinct yet being the same type of thing, as falling
into the same category, of grouping together mind and body in the
way we place chrysanthemums, crocuses, and daffodils into the

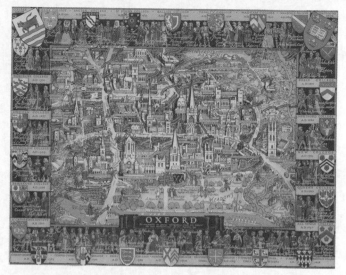

3. Pictorial Map of Oxford University, published in 1948, highlighting Oxford's buildings and grounds. Wondering why the University is not represented as an additional structure would, according to Ryle, be a category mistake.

category of flowers. Ryle called this kind of error a 'category mistake'; Descartes, according to Ryle, was confused about what type of thing the mind is, about what category it falls into.

To illustrate the idea of a category mistake, Ryle asks us to imagine showing a visitor around Oxford University. (Ryle was educated at and spent his academic career at Oxford.) You might show your visitor Christ Church, the Merton playing field, the Radcliffe Camera, the elegant cloisters of New College, and the Bodleian Library in the Old Schools Quadrangle. Now, if, after this tour, your visitor were to ask, 'but where is the university?' your visitor would be seriously confused about what a university is. Oxford University is not something in addition to its buildings and gardens (Figure 3). To place it in the same category as such things—as merely one additional item—is to commit a category mistake.

Of course, in a sense, your visitor is right. If a level five tornado were to rip through campus, sweeping up Oxford's Gothic arches, dreaming spires, and thick stone walls, we could still maintain that the university endures in its students, principles, organizations, and by-laws. However, the idea of Oxford that Ryle had in mind was Oxford as an architectural structure. After an architectural tour, you've seen Oxford (as an architectural structure) since as an architectural structure, Oxford is no more than the aggregate sum of its landscaped gardens and stately edifices. To think otherwise—to think that it is somewhat like one of the buildings, yet hidden in the shadows—is, according to Ryle, like being disappointed at never having met the average family: the one with 2.4 children.

Ryle proposes a test for identifying category mistakes: conjoin the relevant terms with an 'and'; if the result is absurd, a category mistake has been perpetrated. Sometimes such 'mistakes' are intentional. For example, in Charles Dickens's *Pickwick Papers*, the Reverend Mr. Stiggins, after 'having quite as much pineapple rum and water about him as he could comfortably accommodate, took his hat and his leave'; since you don't take your hat in the same way you take your leave, the conjunction illustrates a category mistake. So does the narrator's description of Miss Bolo, who, after becoming exasperated by Mr Pickwick's ineptitude at playing cards, goes 'straight home, in a flood of tears and a sedan chair'.

The type of category mistake that Ryle attributes to dualists, however, is committed unknowingly, and the 'joke' takes a book to explain. But the basic idea can be conveyed briefly. The statement, 'I have a mind and a body,' is absurd because you do not have a mind in the same way that you have a body. Just as a university (as an architectural structure) is not something additional to all its buildings and grounds, the mind, according to Ryle, is not something additional to the workings of the body. There is no inner thought; there is no inner light of consciousness. Rather, thought is simply behaving in characteristically thoughtful ways and consciousness is simply behaving in characteristically conscious ways (you are awake, moving around, responsive, and so forth). So too with your beliefs: when you look out of the window and form the belief that it is raining, you do not have something going on in you that is like a material process, only intangible; rather, according to Ryle, you engage in a set of behaviours: you bring an umbrella and don a raincoat before going outside. Your belief that it is raining just is that set of behaviours. Our actions are analogous to the buildings and grounds of a university while the mind is analogous to the university itself, and the dualist's 'big mistake' is thinking of mind and body as two things that fall under the heading 'parts of a person'.

Though Ryle rejected the appellation, his theory of the mind is often classified as a version of *behaviourism* because it understands the mind as a set of behaviours. According to the behaviourist, there is nothing behind the scenes. What you think is what you do. 'Overt intelligent performances are not clues to the workings of minds,' Ryle writes, 'they *are* those workings.'

Varieties of behaviourism

Behaviourism is a view about the nature of the mind: mental states—beliefs, desires, emotions, and so forth—are sets of *behaviours*. Which behaviours? Those that dualists merely associate with what they refer to as 'mental states'. (Note that such a definition is not circular: mental states are partially defined not in terms of mental states but in terms of the phrase 'mental states'.) For the dualist, intelligence is an inner state that causes a certain type of behaviour (perhaps, asking challenging questions, explaining novel solutions to difficult problems, correcting one's own mistakes, and persevering even after a spate of rejections); in contrast, the behaviourist identifies intelligence with this behaviour.

At least this is how the polysemous term 'behaviourism' is understood in philosophy of mind. Outside of philosophy departments, the theory of behaviourism is generally associated with the views of two 20th-century American psychologists: John B. Watson, who advocated 'methodological behaviourism', which is the precept that the data for psychology must come only from the study of empirically observable behaviour, and B. F. Skinner, who developed 'operant conditioning', which is a system of teaching by administering punishments and rewards. While operant conditioning is still useful for understanding everything from video game addiction to the effectiveness of 'time outs' in childrearing, many psychologists today neither think of themselves as behaviourists nor refrain from investigating memory, attention, and other internal mental states. Nonetheless, most experimental work in psychology is behaviouristic in its methodology. For example, psychologists might compare the performance of runners who were *instructed* to attend to their own movements and runners who were *instructed* to attend to the finish line. While the goal of such a study might be to better understand how the conscious mental process of attention affects running, the study's methodology is behaviouristic as it examines behavioural effects of different kinds of instructions.

Behaviourism (the philosophical theory that mind is behaviour), though distinct from methodological behaviourism, is nonetheless connected to it: if philosophical behaviourism is true and the mind is merely a set of behaviours, methodological behaviourism would be mandated (as there would be nothing of the mind to study besides behaviour). But one can be a methodological behaviourist without accepting that the nature of mind runs only skin deep; one can think that in studying the mind one can only study behaviour without maintaining that the mind just is behaviour.

Other minds and causation

The philosophical theory of behaviourism is motivated, in part,
by the desire to avoid what is referred to as 'the problem of other
minds', which is the problem of specifying how you can know that
anyone other than yourself has a mind. This problem encompasses
a question broached in the Preface: how do I know that when you
see green your experience isn't like the experience I have when
I see red? But it doesn't stop there: how do you know that when
I look at a Granny Smith apple, and exclaim, 'What a brilliant
shade of green!' I'm experiencing anything at all? Ryle maintained
that answering this question was particularly difficult for someone
who thought of the mind along Cartesian lines.

Descartes held that nearly everything is susceptible to doubt. That
you are reading this book? You could be dreaming that you are
reading. That two plus three equals five? Perhaps, some evil
genius (or crazed neuroscientist) has manipulated us all into
thinking that it does, when, in fact, it doesn't. (Is such a situation
even in principle possible? I leave it to you to decide.) But that you
are thinking, Descartes argued, is impervious to doubt because the
very act of doubting is a form of thinking; in doubting that you
are thinking, you are, at the same time, affirming to yourself that
you are in fact doing so. Of the contents of our minds, he argued,
we have direct and indubitable knowledge. And from this
indubitability, he established his own existence: *cogito, ergo sum*.

When it comes to understanding other people, however, we have
knowledge only of their actions—what they do and say—and
although we assume that other people have inner lives that guide
their actions, their inner lives can never be observed by us directly.
'The workings of one mind', as Ryle put it, explaining Descartes's
view, 'are not witnessable by other observers; its career is private.'

Of course, there are indirect clues to others' minds. According to
Descartes, the inner mind has outward effects: a parched feeling

in your throat (a feeling which, according to Descartes, occurs in your mind) will cause you to reach for a glass of water. Yet how can we know that this causal connection occurs in others? How can we know that the cause of someone else's reaching for water, or even saying that they are thirsty, has anything to do with their inner experience of thirst? You know that when you venture to the water fountain, you do so because you feel thirsty, and you know that other people's behaviour and neurophysiology are very similar to yours. Thus, you may be tempted to conclude that the cause of their behaviour is very similar to yours. Yet, this reasoning proceeds by generalizing from only one case: your own experience. Generalizing from one case would seem to be a classic example of what philosophers deride as a 'hasty generalization'. How do you know that you're not unique?

Descartes had an answer to this question: we can know that others have minds because God would not deceive us into thinking that they do when they in fact are mere automatons. But behaviourists are not satisfied with a *deus ex machina* solution to the other minds problem. Not only is it difficult to discern the intentions of the All-Powerful, but behaviourists prefer to not lean on Him/Her/Them in philosophical explanations at all. And they don't need to, since behaviourism, in contrast to dualism, doesn't have a problem of other minds. By equating the mind with behaviour, behaviourists can straightforwardly determine whether others have minds: if they act intelligently, they are intelligent; if they act waggishly, they are waggish, and so forth. Nothing is hidden from view; when it comes to feelings that we typically think *elicit* vocalizations, in the way that pain prompts your cry of 'ouch!', behaviourism implies that your friends can readily know what you are feeling since the feeling just is the exclamation.

Not only does behaviourism skirt the problem of other minds, it also avoids Princess Elisabeth's objection: that an immaterial, unextended mind cannot come in causal contact with an extended body. If, as the behaviourist holds, the mind is nothing more than

24

the body in action, then (even on the assumption that causation requires contact) there is no gap between mind and body that requires bridging. True enough, mind and body could still be understood as falling into different categories: the one, the body, is a thing in the world, and the other, the mind, is something that that thing does. Yet to explain how, say, bodily damage causes us to feel pain (which on the behaviourist's picture is merely the characteristic behaviour associated with bodily damage), the behaviourist need only refer to anatomical and physiological processes: tissue damage, enervated nerves, muscle contractions, and so forth.

Finally, behaviourism avoids Ryle's own take on the dualist's difficulty with causation. Although Ryle does not argue that a dualist account of the mind precludes the mind from causally interacting with the body, he does think that if dualism were true, the causal force that mediates pin pricks and pain would need to be a strange hybrid: neither immaterial nor material, neither accessible to introspection nor amenable to scientific investigation, neither of the mind nor of the body; if dualism were true, he tells us, causal relations could be nothing other than 'theoretical shuttlecocks which are forever being bandied from the physiologist to the psychologist and from the psychologist back to the physiologist'. Behaviourism, in contrast, needs no such bandying as the psychologist is simply a rarefied physiologist.

Super-spartans

Despite behaviourism's ostensible advantages over dualism, many have felt that it is an untenable theory, that seeing the mind as behaviour is like judging a book by its cover: it leaves out everything that matters. To understand why, consider a world in which it is the pinnacle of bad manners to reveal that you are in pain. From a very young age, you are taught that yelling 'ouch', gritting your teeth, or otherwise showing any indication of feeling pain is uncouth and impermissible. Furthermore, imagine that in this world everyone has developed the ability to suppress their reactions to pain at will. When a migraine hits, you go to work rather than spending the afternoon lying down in a quiet, dark room; when you break a bone, you'll be rushed to the emergency room to have it set, but along the way you'll gab casually with the ambulance team. In this imagined world, people feel pain—when in pain, they may calmly report that, yes, indeed, they are feeling pain—but they suppress all typical pain behaviours.

Hilary Putnam, the 20th-century American philosopher who originated this thought experiment, points out that the existence of such 'super-spartans' throws behaviourism into question yet does not refute it since behaviourists identify the mind in terms of both behaviours and *dispositions* to behave. As Ryle explains his view, when we describe people's mental characteristics, 'we are not referring to occult episodes of which their overt acts and utterances are effects'; rather, we are referring either to 'those overt acts and utterances themselves' or to a 'disposition, or a complex of dispositions'. When Margo is upset at her spouse for misloading the dishwasher, she is a spartan inasmuch as she keeps it to herself, but she's nonetheless disposed to say something. And the same could be said of super-spartans' pain behaviour: they are still disposed to cry 'ouch'. Moreover, the super-spartans hide their pain only for the most part, since, when asked, they may admit to feeling pain. And, for the behaviourist, speaking the sentence 'I am in pain', or even responding 'Yes' to the question 'Are you in pain?', is a form of pain-behaviour. Thus, the super-spartans are not examples of people who can feel pain without evincing pain behaviour, and so the world of super-spartans does not break behaviourism.

But perhaps the super-spartans are not as spartan as they could be. Imagine another world: a super-super-spartan world, in which the social mores prohibiting pain-behaviour are so extreme that the inhabitants of this world, far from being disposed to express their pain, are disposed to cover it up. Individuals in this world may think that kidney-stone pain is intolerable; however, neither would they reveal this, nor would they be disposed to reveal this. Nonetheless, Putnam suggests, they could know what pain is and know when they've got it. If this scenario makes sense, then behaviourism is indeed untenable.

But does it make sense? Would the inhabitants of such a community know what the word 'pain' means? If in order to understand a term, one must understand how it is used in a community, then since neither the term 'pain' nor any synonymous words or phrases are used in the super-super-spartan world, it might be argued that super-super-spartans could not even think that they are in pain, as the concept of pain would have no meaning for them.

Ryle's teacher, Ludwig Wittgenstein, devised a thought experiment that is sometimes interpreted as showing that the super-super spartan scenario is incoherent. Wittgenstein asks us to imagine a community where everyone carries a box, which they treat as containing something; it could be anything, but let's call it a 'beetle'. Since you never get to peer inside anyone else's box, you cannot know first-hand that the contents of your box are like the contents of anyone else's nor even that other people's boxes contain anything at all. Nonetheless, people in this community could learn to say such things as 'my beetle is hungry right now', or 'such a cute little beetle my darling's becoming' and to respond appropriately upon hearing such phrases. One conclusion to draw from this thought experiment is that our ability to converse about beetles depends on external social interactions and behaviour, and has nothing to do with what is inside our box; the beetle, as Wittgenstein puts it, drops out of the equation. And the same, Wittgenstein suggests, goes for the term 'pain': its meaning is not determined by an inner feeling—the beetle—but can only acquire meaning through publicly observable behaviour. If Wittgenstein's account of linguistic meaning is correct—if there could be no 'private language', no language that refers to something that only you have access to—there could be no super-super-spartan world.

In the Preface, I suggested that thought experiments in philosophy are intended to be pellucid and univocal. Yet Wittgenstein's beetle-in-a box thought experiment is, perhaps intentionally, multivocal. Thus, I leave it to you to decipher and to determine whose argument is preferable: Putnam's argument that behaviourism makes no sense because super-super-spartanism is possible or Wittgenstein's argument—if this is in fact his point—that the term 'pain' acquires meaning only by its use in a community?

Dispositions

According to some, the behaviourist confronts a foe more formidable than the spartans, no matter how super they may be. This foe is the problem of making sense of the behaviouristic conception of dispositions. What is a disposition? It seems that if you are disposed to cry out in pain when hurt, then you have a tendency to do so. Yet tendencies seem rather more internal and invisible than behaviour, rather like the Cartesian mind that Ryle ridicules.

The behaviourist's response is that dispositions are merely certain sets of true conditional, or 'if-then', statements: all that is meant in saying that you are disposed to cry 'ouch' is that the sentence 'if you had the ability to cry "ouch", then you would' is true. For example, consider the terrifying affliction known as 'locked-in syndrome'. Individuals with locked-in syndrome are, it is thought, fully conscious yet unable to move or express themselves in any way whatsoever; they may experience terror but are unable to show it. This may seem to present a challenge for behaviourism. Yet if dispositions are merely certain sets of true if-then statements, a behaviourist can say that when locked-in individuals are terrified, they are disposed to tremble; in other words, it is true that if they were not locked-in, then they would tremble.

And yet, one might wonder what makes the behaviourist's if-then statements true? What makes the sentence 'if the glass were dropped, it would shatter' true is that glass has a disordered amorphous structure. Analogously, it seems that if it's true that a locked-in individual is terrified, then something—other than behaviour—must make it true that they are terrified. What this something is, however, is not of interest to behaviourists since for behaviourists, the feeling of terror just is the behaviour or the disposition to behave in certain ways; what grounds the behaviours and dispositions is irrelevant, as they see it, to the question of whether someone experiences terror.

A compromise view

While Putnam's thought experiment attempts to discredit behaviourism by illustrating the possibility of an internal sensation without its characteristic behaviour, one might instead argue that behavior typically associated with a particular internal sensation may occur sans the sensation. Stanislavsky method-acting notwithstanding, actors behave as if they are in pain, without feeling pain. Of course, dramatized pain does not entirely resemble the real thing: when the curtain lowers on Henrik Ibsen's *Ghosts*, Mrs Alving, a normally articulate woman, is left clutching a bottle of morphine pills screaming, 'No, no, no!...Yes!...No, no!'; yet, within seconds, the actor is smiling as she takes her bow. Someone who is actually tormented would not smile so readily. Indeed, the behaviourist could argue that the actor playing Mrs Alving, although she is acting as if she were tormented, is not *disposed* to act as if she were; acting, as the 18th-century French philosopher and art critic Denis Diderot remarked, is not natural; rather than being disposed to behave as they do on stage, actors must deliberately present themselves in such ways so as to have the desired effect on the audience.

These responses notwithstanding, many still find a behaviouristic account of pain and other sensations implausible. But what about intelligence? When people say that they are in severe bodily pain, as long as they are not trying to deceive us, we generally accept what they say. To put this in philosophy-speak, pain—bodily pain, though not necessarily psychological pain—seems to be something that we have 'first-person authority' over: you know better than anyone else does whether you are experiencing a headache or back-pain. As first-person authority is sometimes explained, if you think you are in pain, you are in pain. Yet, the idea that if you think you are smart, then you are smart, is not nearly as compelling; for although it wouldn't be very nice, it at least makes sense to say to someone, 'You may think you are intelligent, but you're not.' Indeed, if we are to take Socrates as our model, the true sign of wisdom is thinking that one knows nothing.

It is not clear that a super-super-spartan thought experiment could refute behaviourism about intelligence. Imagine an individual, whom I'll call Z, who shows no signs of being a genius; Z, let us say, has been extensively tested but performs below, sometimes even far below, average in all cognitive skills, and just in case Z suffers from test anxiety, let us say that Z has, since birth, been secretly observed and has given no sign of being able to perform complex cognitive tasks. Is it reasonable to think that Z might nonetheless be a genius? If you ask Z, 'Are you smart?' Z will say—while, perhaps, trying to open a pickle jar with a monkey wrench—'Yes, I'm very smart.' But, in contrast to pain, Z, arguably, is not the authority on this. Perhaps with intelligence, what you do is what you are: if you don't act intelligently, then you aren't intelligent.

An early formulation of behaviourism about intelligence can be found in the writings of the 19th-century German philosopher Georg Wilhelm Friedrich Hegel: 'when a person's performance and inner possibility, capacity or intention are contrasted', he tells us, 'it is the former alone which is to be regarded as true'. In determining intelligence, we must look at performance, not inner light. Hegel also warns us to not fall into believing those who claim to be something other than what their actions reveal, and he finds the braggart who 'fancies that in this inner self he is something else than what he is in the deed' particularly annoying, as does that Supreme Behaviourist who advises, 'by their fruits ye shall know them'.

Indeed, in contrast to the inner-light theory, a behaviourist account of intelligence might be not only theoretically, but also practically preferable. Research conducted by the contemporary philosopher Sarah-Jane Leslie and her colleagues indicates that when it comes to making hiring decisions, philosophers tend to value 'raw intelligence', and they value it more than other academics value it. This value, she argues, may in part account for why women and minorities are underrepresented in philosophy since in making decisions based on whether an individual is brilliant in the inner-light sense, one is readily influenced by inaccurate stereotypes. In contrast, disciplines that tend to rely more on achievement (behaviour) tend to have more equitable hiring practices.

Deeming people unintelligent because they fail to act in a certain way, however, raises its own set of problems. For a child who hasn't been blessed with a proper education, a simple behaviouristic account of intelligence that aligns intelligence exclusively with performance may not issue the correct ruling. And there is another problem: it is not at all clear what behaviours should count as capturing intelligence. Perhaps exceptional musicians or dancers should be considered highly intelligent regardless of how they perform on conventional tests of intelligence. Moreover, what indicates you're savvy in one culture might indicate just the opposite in another. The behaviourist can respond to the first problem by contextualizing their concept of behaviour: it's not the behaviour per se that matters, but behaviour relative to the environment. The second problem is rather more vexed.

What about other mental states? Ying claims that she strongly desires to improve her chess game. But if she never reviews past games, memorizes openings, or plays frequently, we might be inclined to think that she is mistaken about what she wants. Raj thinks he's shy, but we know he's not because of his outgoing behaviour. Your manager is convinced she's witty, but she's wrong because she never makes witty remarks. That desire, shyness, wittiness may be understood by well-informed observers better than by those undergoing them, is what a behaviourist theory of mind would predict.

However, if behaviourism is a viable account of only some of our mental processes, it requires supplementation. And if one rejects dualism, one needs another theory of mind to serve this ancillary purpose.

Chapter 3
Physicalism

It is currently thought that the universe began about 13.7 billion years ago, expanding out from a tiny point of near infinite density. Within a mere 10^{-43} seconds, in an unfathomably hot environment, the fundamental forces began to separate—with gravity in the lead quickly followed by the strong, weak, and electromagnetic forces. A millionth of a second in, during a brief but vigorous period of continual rearrangement, quarks aggregated into nucleons, and within around one to ten minutes, the temperature dropped too low to allow further neutron production and simple nuclei were formed. It took around 380,000 years before the first atoms were formed. These early atoms were almost exclusively hydrogen and helium, which, in large numbers, fell together due to gravity to create the brilliant nucleosynthetic factories (stars) that produced all the other elements in the periodic table. And by around the 9.2-billion-year mark, the solar system was formed. Life on earth is thought to have begun within a billion years after that, perhaps arising in undersea alkaline vents, and within a couple billion more years eukaryotic cells evolved, with multicellular life developing in another billion years or so. Hundreds of millions of years later—approximately 4 million years ago—humans began to evolve along the verdant savannas of east Africa.

Where in this picture does the mind make its appearance? If we were to carefully examine each step of the progression from the birth of the universe to the existence of human life on earth, would we find that minds were an extra ingredient, added to the universe around the time sentient creatures evolved? Or did the complexity of the brain bring minds into the picture for free? Or might it be that mental forces—albeit in a primitive form— were around since the beginning?

In the broadest terms, the philosophical theory of physicalism maintains that the explanation for how minds came about is no different from the explanation for how rivers, trees, mountains and meadows came about. Mind was not something extra, added at the beginning or somewhere along the way; rather, from the stock of basic physical ingredients that make up a human—mostly oxygen, hydrogen, nitrogen, carbon, calcium and phosphorus—all that was required was the cooking.

Physicalism—sometimes referred to as 'materialism'—stands in stark opposition to Descartes's dualism, which maintains that the immaterial mind, or soul, is an additional ingredient, brought into the world by God at the moment of conception. According to Descartes, in contrast to the introduction of the mind, the emergence of all other features of the sublunar world admits scientific explanation. Indeed, in the *Passions of the Soul*, Descartes even aims to provide a scientific explanation for the way in which the soul, once introduced, joins the body: the heart's warm blood, he hypothesizes, causes the soul to love the body ('c'est a dire l'aymoit'), entwining the two until the body loses its heat at death, whereupon the soul loses interest. God wasn't needed to join the soul to the body; thermal energy was attractive enough. However, God was needed to create the soul, which makes Descartes's dualism contrary to physicalism.

For the physicalist, a divine helping hand comes in neither at the beginning of the universe, with God setting mental particles into motion along with the non-mental ones, nor somewhere along the way, with God adding minds at conception. The physicalist thinks that, although our knowledge of the creation and evolution of the universe is incomplete, we know enough to know that God isn't working behind the scenes. Everything that exists today—including human minds—came about, according to the physicalist, in virtue of the rearrangements of and interactions between the physical particles and forces that emerged after the universe's birth. In response to Napoleon's question about the place of God in his 1796 theory of the origins of the solar system, the French mathematician Pierre-Simon Laplace allegedly declared, 'I have no need for that hypothesis'; the physicalist, too, has no need for God to explain how consciousness came into the world. The world, according to the physicalist, consists of nothing but physical things and forces.

From behaviourism to the identity theory

Physicalism is a theory about the general nature of the world; it asserts that everything—from particles to people, from multi-star systems to multiplayer video games—is physical. And since the mind is seen as physicalism's greatest nemesis, the central challenge for physicalists is to show how the mind sits comfortably in the physical world.

How might this task be accomplished? One theory that aims to provide a physical account of the mind was introduced in the previous chapter: behaviourism. According to the behaviourist, the mind is understood in terms of one's behaviour. Intelligence is not some inner light making us solve differential equations and recite passages of poetry. Rather it is simply the doing of these things, or at least having the propensity to do them given the appropriate circumstances. Since the behaviour you engage in when solving differential equations or reciting poetry comprises exclusively physical movements of the body, behaviourism is a form of physicalism.

We saw in the last chapter, however, that although behaviourism may be a plausible account of some mental states, many philosophers think that it is not a plausible account of *all* mental states. Putnam, recall, argued that one might stifle one's pain behaviour, possibly even to such a degree that one is not even inclined to reveal it. In general, behaviourism is thought to leave out a crucial aspect of the mind, namely, our ability to experience our own mental states from a first-person point of view.

The British-Australian philosopher J. J. C. Smart wrote in 1959 of another potential problem for behaviourism: not all mental states are associated with characteristic behaviours. Consider what occurs when you experience a yellowish-orange after-image—the kind of thing you might experience after staring at a bright blue light. Such experiences, Smart argues, are not associated with any characteristic behaviour—for example, you probably won't always or perhaps will never try to grab it, nor will you be disposed to do this. If the perception of after-images is not associated with any characteristic behaviour, and if perceptions of after-images are some of the furniture of the mind, behaviourism cannot be a full account of mentality.

How ought we to understand after-images? While the dualist will say that after-images are something immaterial, Smart understands them as brain processes. My experience of seeing a yellowish-orange after-image is identical to, is one and the same thing as, neural activity in my skull. Indeed, according to Smart's 'identity theory', sensory experiences are brain processes. After stubbing your toe, you might feel as if the pain you experience is in your toe, but according to the identity theory, you'd be wrong. According to the identity theory, the pain is in your brain since pain just *is* a certain type of neural activity. A neurosurgeon peering into your skull could see your pain—not merely the neural processes that cause your pain, but the pain itself—and could touch it with a scalpel. And if the pain were so blinding that it caused you to see stars, then (since the experience of seeing stars

is, on the identity theory, something that goes on in the brain)
the neurosurgeon, in observing your brain, could also see your
experience of those stars.

The concept of identity in question is *numerical* identity: the
neural processes a neurosurgeon might see (call them 'n-processes')
are one and the same thing as your experience of pain in the sense
that C♯ and D♭ are one and the same key on the piano. Although
the context in which we use the terms or phrases may differ, a C♯
key cannot exist on a complete keyboard without a corresponding
D♭ (and vice versa); similarly, the identity theorist claims, pain
cannot exist without n-processes (and vice versa).

Support for the identity theory comes in part from analogies to
successful scientific reductions. Because science has revealed that
lightning is nothing more than electrical discharge, water nothing
more than H_2O, and the gene nothing more than DNA, there is
good reason to think, the identity theorist argues, that science will
one day reveal that yellowish-orange after-images and sundry
other mental processes are nothing more than brain states.

Such analogical reasoning is bolstered, according to Smart, by
'Ockham's razor', a heuristic for scientific practice—named after
the 14th-century Franciscan friar William of Ockham, who is
thought to have originated the idea—telling us that when there
are two (or more) theories that account for the empirical data, we
should prefer the simpler theory. For example, Copernicus'
heliocentric model of the solar system and Ptolemy's geocentric
model both made accurate predictions about the movement of
celestial bodies. However, the geocentric model was, in many
ways, more complicated, with its numerous sub-epicycles and
non-uniform planetary orbits. Thus, an application of Ockham's
razor leads us to the Copernican model of the solar system.
According to Smart, Ockham's razor should similarly lead us to
prefer the identity theory over dualism, as dualism would require
additional scientific laws linking immaterial sensations to brain

processes. Such laws, he says, are unlike any we know; they have 'a queer "smell" to them' and are better done without.

Smart's argument is successful, of course, only if the analogies are apt, and some argue that they aren't because the mind is significantly different from lightning, water, the gene, and other purportedly reduced entities. Yet the identity theorist sees this objection as dogmatic. There are certainly differences between the mind and such things. Not only is anything different from any other thing, but the mind may be more complex than lightning, water, and the like. But none of this, the identity theorist argues, indicates that a reduction is impossible. Indeed, they point out, we are getting closer to reducing mind to brain every day. Scientists have found that individuals who are depressed have reduced levels of the neurotransmitter serotonin, that schizophrenia seems to be correlated with disruptions in the neurotransmitters dopamine, glutamate, and norepinephrine (noradrenaline), that disruptions in the prefrontal cortex's ability to communicate with other areas of the brain undergird obsessive-compulsive disorder. To be sure, we are still far from fully understanding mental illness in neurological terms, but identity theorists think that we are close enough to be confident that mental illness as well as all other mental processes are reducible to, are nothing other than, localized or distributed neural processes.

Dualists, of course, reject the identity theory. But you can reject the identity theory without accepting dualism. A physicalist might counter Smart by arguing that his purported examples of reductions aren't actually examples of reductions; they aren't examples of cases in which two apparently distinct things are actually one and the same thing. There are many cases of electrical discharge that are not cases of lightning—the spark between your finger and the doorknob, the sparks generated by a dust storm or a Van de Graaff generator, the reddish-orange flashes in the upper atmosphere, called 'sprites'. Similarly, a glass of water includes substances that are not H_2O—North American tap water typically contains calcium, magnesium sodium, and other minerals in addition to H_2O—and although we say that the Great Salt Lake is a body of water, a human baby is composed of a higher percentage of H_2O. Furthermore, even if there were blocks of ice so pure that they comprised nothing but H_2O, if you asked for a glass of water and were given only this ice, you'd be justifiably disappointed. And as for the identity between the gene and DNA, long sequences of DNA lie between genes. Strictly speaking at least, the standard examples identity theorists provide as examples of successful reductions are not actually reductions and thus cannot serve to illustrate the mind–brain identity theorist's claim.

To be sure, identity theorists will respond that when they draw an analogy between mind–brain reduction and, say, the reduction of genes to DNA, they are merely speaking in an abbreviated manner and that the correct analogue would be much more complex. Yet once the complexities are spelled out, internecine squabbles may arise among scientists; for example, there is a debate over whether the gene reduces exclusively to the sequence of DNA transcribed to RNA or to all of the DNA involved in this transcription process, including enhancers and promoters that might be completely separated from the sequence being transcribed. And such squabbles may vitiate the identity theorist's claim that one need only look to science to illuminate the way in which the mind is reducible to the brain.

Multiple realization

Consider how different a human brain is from an octopus's brain, or rather, *brains*—the Giant Pacific Octopus has one central brain as well as brains in each of its eight arms. An octopus's neural structure enables it to attack prey, perceive its environment, and even solve mazes. Yet the way it does differs from the way our brains allow us to hunt, perceive, and problem solve. If pain is identified as neural activity in specific regions of a human brain, and octopuses brains were to lack those regions, the identity theorists would need to conclude that octopuses cannot feel pain. And this is a conclusion that many are not willing to accept.

The thought that octopuses and other creatures may share some of our mental states without sharing our underlying neural states, has led to the view that mental states are 'multiply realizable'. The multiple realization of pain, for example, means that in different species, the same kind of pain can have different neural signatures. Since Smart's identity theory does not permit multiple realization, the identity theory, it is argued, must be wrong.

Identity theorists, however, have their own analysis of the situation. Yes, the neural signature of pain will show up differently in different species, but when the neuroscientific account is complete, we will find that such so-called 'different' neural states are structurally similar enough to count as the same kind of state. Whereas my brain may light up on the right side of my head and the octopuses' brains may light up along their left arms, what is going on will still be similar enough to count as one and the same kind of brain process. Or the identity theorist might argue that octopus pain itself is likely quite different from human pain so one would expect it to have a different neural signature. In fact, one would expect different kinds of pains—sharp pain, dull pain, heat pain—to have different neural signatures even within the same person. Thus, the identity theory still stands.

Or does it? Some argue that even if the identity theory were able to account for pain in humans, cephalopods, and all other creatures, great and small, on this planet, the identity theory is nonetheless challenged by the possibility of creatures elsewhere in this universe that behave as if they are in pain yet possess nothing in their brains, if they have brains at all, that could reasonably count as the same kind of processes that occurs in earthy creatures when we experience pain. The identity theory implies that such extraterrestrials are incapable of feeling the types of pains we feel.

Yet, if these individuals were to behave as we do when we suffer, treating them as they were insentient, some argue, cannot feel pain would be immoral.

But what if we are alone in this vast universe? Some philosophers argue that the identity theory may be challenged by even the mere possibility of conscious, pain-experiencing extraterrestrials with brains full of intricate swirls of green goop, or, for that matter, by artificially created computer minds. Critics of the identity theory argue that the theory could not account for either of these types of minds. Such critics do not necessarily want to give up physicalism; they merely want a physical theory of the mind that can allow for pain and other mental states to be realized in human brains, octopus arms, alien goop, computer processing units, and sundry other things.

Perhaps one might say that human pain is identical to the pain-relevant brain areas in humans, octopus pain identical to the pain-relevant (extended) brain areas in octopuses, alien pain to green goop, and so forth. But what makes these disparate bodily features all count as pain? The natural answer is that they all hurt, but the identity theorist doesn't have hurtfulness as a distinct concept that can be called upon to explain what makes alien goop, the pain-relevant brain areas in humans, and so forth all count as pain. Something more, it seems, needs to be said.

Functionalism

Functionalism is a theory of mind that allows for the multiple realization of mental states and says something about why pain-relevant brain areas in humans, pain-relevant (extended) brain areas in octopuses, and alien green goop can all be associated with pain. With respect to pain, functionalism, on one incarnation of the theory (there are many incarnations) is the view that pain is whatever substrate—be it grey neural matter or green goop—that reacts to bodily damage (that unfortunate smashing of the toe when you stubbed it) and causes pain behaviour (cursing, perhaps) and other mental states (such as the belief that you are in pain), states which are themselves given a functional description. On another incarnation of the view, the causal network is specified in terms of neuronal activity. Of course, the causal network that pain mediates is highly complex, as pain can be caused by a multitude of factors and can lead to a multitude of effects. The key idea of functionalism—and a common denominator of both these accounts—is that pain is at the centre of a causal network.

This key idea can be understood in terms of a detective story. A detective may uncover many details about a murder: Squire D was found dead in his country home at 11 PM traces of poison were found on his lips; the back door that leads directly to the kitchen seems to have been broken into after the housekeeper left at 10 PM fingerprints that belong to neither Squire D nor the housekeeper were found on D's teacup, which also tested positive for cyanide; fresh footprints of size 11 shoes were found leading from the back door and across the street. The detective, then, is looking for an individual that can fit the clues, an individual with size 11 shoes, fingerprints with a pattern that matches those found on the teacup, a familiarity with cyanide, and no alibi for the time of the murder. Just as the murderer (whoever it turns out to be) must fit this description, pain (whether activity in area p, area q, or in green goop) must fit a certain description that specifies what it does: it's what causes screams, is caused by certain types of bodily damage, and can cause other mental states, such as anger at the person causing you pain. In other words, pain, according to the functionalist, is whatever satisfies a certain story, or 'causal role'. While the identity theory says that pain is the neural realization of this role in humans, functionalism leaves the realization open: pain is whatever fits the story.

While philosophers who refer to themselves as functionalists are typically also physicalists, functionalism, itself, is neutral between physicalist and non-physicalist accounts of the mind. Functionalism is a form of physicalism when the state that mediates the input of bodily damage and the output of a scream is a physical state, such as a brain state. But the theory of functionalism does not preclude the immaterial soul from being identified as the murderer, as it were. Thus, if humans have immaterial souls, a functionalist account of pain would specify that pain is the state of the soul that is caused by bodily damage and causes one to scream and to believe that one is in pain.

Functionalism markets itself as taking what is best of both behaviourism and the identity theory, borrowing the idea that mental states are closely connected to our behaviour from behaviourism and the idea that the mind is an internal state from the identity theory. Functionalists also think that their view leaves behind what is wrong with these theories: in contrast to behaviourism, the connection between mentality and behaviour is not so tight as to preclude the experience of after-images from counting as mental states, and in contrast to the identity theory, functionalism allows for extraterrestrial and artificial minds. Because of these virtues, the functional account of the mind is quite popular among philosophers.

Chauvinism and liberalism

Despite its popularity, the degree to which functionalism has a tentacle up over behaviourism and the identity theory has been questioned. According to the American philosopher Ned Block, functionalism's advantage over competing theories is tempered by the fact that functionalism is too liberal: although it allows for the multiple realization of mental states in a way that the identity theory does not, it ends up attributing mental states to things that, as he sees it, clearly do not have them.

Imagine a future in which the world's greatly expanded population is ruled by a single leader, the world-nation leader, and imagine that this leader decrees that for one hour on 1 January, the nation will celebrate the new year by enacting the functional program for joy: around 100 billion people will carry out the job of neurons by firing off text messages to other neurons (people) at a rate of five to fifty messages per second, while another 80 billion or so people take on supporting roles as glial cells, the cells that hold neurons in place and help them function as the should. For this one hour, all of humanity will be acting in a way that is isomorphic, in relevant respects, to the firing patterns of the brain cells of someone experiencing joy. At the height of the celebration, the world leader, who had been a mere observer of the activity, undergoes an operation in which their brain is removed and all of their sensory and motor nerve endings are set up via wi-fi to receive output and provide input to this nation-brain. If functionalism is true, the world leader would now feel joy. Block argues, however, that this is absurd. Not only do none of the individuals performing the tasks, which are exceedingly dull, experience joy, but, according to Block, nations, even world-nations connected to their leader's body, are not the type of things that could count as, or be the functional realization of, joy. Thus functionalism, Block argues, is guilty of liberalism.

Furthermore, any adjustment to the theory a functionalist might make to avoid liberalism, Block argues—by, perhaps, specifying that the communication between 'neurons' be carried out by not only electrical signals but also by chemical neurotransmitters— will lead to a theory that is guilty of 'chauvinism', a theory that will fail to attribute joy or other mental properties to creatures that clearly have them. Even the functional account that allowed for a world-nation to give rise to joy might unduly exclude creatures without anything that is functionally isomorphic to neurons and glial cells from such happiness.

Is functionalism, no matter how it's understood, unable to avoid the Scylla and Charybdis of chauvinism and liberalism? Might the world-nation actually have a mind? Might there be a functional theory of mental states that is properly discriminating without being discriminatory, a theory that hits the sweet spot, a Goldilocks theory that is neither too abstract nor too specific? Philosophers cross swords over these questions.

Mysterianism and eliminativism

For physicalists that both reject the identity theory and think that functionalism will leave Goldilocks wanting, there are other options. For example, so-called 'mysterians' think that mentality is physical but also that it is beyond our ken to know how it is physical; mental concepts and physical concepts are so radically different, mysterians maintain, that we can't conceive of how the mind could be a lump of grey matter even though it is such a lump. Others think that the reason we can't account for mentality in physical terms is that our concept of mentality is hopelessly confused; in fact, they think that it is so hopelessly confused that it ought to be jettisoned. This view is referred to as 'eliminativism'. The world is entirely physical, says the eliminativist, yet there is no need to figure out how the mind fits into the physical world since the mind does not exist.

It might seem odd to deny the existence of the mind. And, in fact, only the most extreme versions of eliminativism do this. The more moderate eliminativists argue merely that in studying the mind we need to leave open the possibility that some of what we currently think of as aspects of our mind might not exist. Consider hysteria. The signs and symptoms of hysteria have varied through the ages and across cultures, but it has frequently been thought of as primarily a female affliction, caused by a prior trauma, affecting one's ability to enjoy sex. In 1980, hysteria was removed from the *Diagnostic and Statistical Manual of Mental Disorders* (*DSM*).

We no longer believe that the affliction of hysteria exists. Thus, eliminativism is the correct account of hysteria. The illness of hysteria was eliminated from the *DSM* because the concept was seen as incoherent. The eliminativist thinks that a mature neuroscience will reveal that at least some mental concepts we use today are as confused as the concept of hysteria and ought to similarly be jettisoned. Eliminativists do not wipe the mind out entirely: they generally think that some mental concepts will be usefully reduced to neurological states. But those that can't be are generally seen as having no place in an accurate theory of the mind.

Eliminativists point to our paltry scientific understanding of so many aspects of what we currently think of as the mind. For example, we don't know why we dream. Will we figure this out one day? Not if, as some argue, the concept of dreaming makes no sense. Although we can usefully discuss what goes on in the brain during different sleep stages, perhaps dreaming, like hysteria, doesn't exist; we can talk about activity in the right inferior lingual gyrus, but not about dreaming. Memory is also seen by some as a troubling concept. In everyday discourse, we talk of people having spatial memories, memories for names, fuzzy memories, and even false memories. Is there is some one thing, memory, to which all these phrases refer? Eliminativist about memory think that there isn't and, thus, to understand how the mind actually works, we should revise the concept or even do away with it altogether.

The contemporary Canadian-American philosopher Patricia Churchland, who argues that understanding the details of how the brain works is crucially important to understanding the mind, offers a bevy of analogies to illustrate how scientific discoveries can instigate conceptual change. For example, we once thought that flammable objects contained phlogiston, a substance that was thought to be released during combustion. Experiments showing that burning certain objects fails to make them lighter and in fact makes them heavier (because burning adds oxygen) put the phlogiston theory of combustion and the concept of phlogiston to rest. For centuries it was thought that impetus was an inner force that kept moving objects in motion. Yet Newtonian mechanics had no use for such a force. The vital spirit that was once thought of as necessary for the life was not reduced to DNA but was seen as a mistaken posit and eliminated. Churchland argues that in studying the mind we ought to remember that neuroscience may also instigate conceptual change.

Churchland's focus is our 'folk psychological' concepts, the concepts we standardly use to explain why we do certain things. For example, according to folk psychology, I might say that you picked up a glass of water because you felt thirsty, desired to drink some water, and believed that it was yours to drink. Such an explanation of your action in terms of your feelings, desires, and beliefs might seem plausible. However, the eliminativist thinks that ultimately it will not be coherent. Sometimes you want things but don't act on those wants; sometimes beliefs about how you ought to go about doing something don't guide your actions. Some explanations of our actions in terms of beliefs and desires, Churchland contends, may one day be replaced by neural explanations.

Indeed, Churchland points out, neuroscientific accounts of brain processes have already in some cases replaced explanations of our actions in terms of free will. She cites the 2003 case of a Virginian man who, with no criminal history, sexually molested his 8-year-old stepdaughter and began to compulsively collect child pornography. Because his aberrant behaviour disappeared after the removal of a brain tumour, which was in a region of the brain that regulates sexual behaviour, it makes little sense, she argues, to think of his actions as emanating from his own free will. And since the sex drive in a healthy person is regulated by hormones, we can infer, she suggests, that no one is entirely free to choose to engage in sex. Although neuroscience points to a centre of self-control in the brain, it is unlikely, she argues, that it will ever point to anything like what we currently think of as 'the will'.

Churchland also argues that progress in neurology is precipitating a better understanding of what we think of as the self. Pondering whether an image of her brain is an image of her true self, she answers that in a way it is since there is nothing more to the self than the brain, but also that in a way it's not since the narrative our brains produce about ourselves encompasses much more than the brain. The 18th-century Scottish philosopher David Hume takes the conceptual revision of the self one step further, arguing that what we think of as the self is nothing other than a bundle of perceptions, perceptions of 'heat or cold, light or shade, love or hatred, pain or pleasure'. What happens to us in a dreamless sleep, a time when all perceptions cease? Hume's answer is that without perceptions, we 'may truly be said not to exist'.

Intelligence, some argue, may be another conception that we would be better off without. Rather than accepting either the inner-light or behaviourist theories of intelligence of the sort touched on in Chapter 2, perhaps intelligence does not exist at all.

Other eliminativists think that conscious experiences, such as the feeling of pain, the experience of seeing red, or the taste of a strawberry—what are sometimes referred to as 'qualia'—ought to go the way of phlogiston, arguing that they are illusions. We can, they argue, be mistaken about sensations. For example, the thermal grill illusion (which takes place when you touch a grill of alternating warm and cool bars and experience them as burning hot) seems to show that we can easily mistake our feeling of warmth interspersed with coolness for extreme heat. Moreover, as Daniel Dennett points out, any report of a mental state is made slightly after that mental state has occurred since it takes some time to vocalize the thought, and this leaves room for misremembering what occurred. Since it takes time to think the thought, 'I am in pain', rather than accurately remembering what has just occurred we may be merely creating the idea that we had a feeling of pain (a feeling we didn't actually have).

But even if we are occasionally mistaken, does it make sense to think that we could be radically mistaken about the contents of our minds? Some see eliminativism as self-contradictory since the theory presupposes the existence of the mind: eliminativists must at least *believe* that eliminativism is true. If so, beliefs exist and thus eliminativism about beliefs must be false. Yet, according to eliminativists, the 'belief' that eliminativism is true is nothing more than an assertion that minds don't exist, and this assertion, they hold, is not mental but neurophysiological.

The causal argument for physicalism

While each version of physicalism—the identity theory, functionalism, mysterianism, and eliminativism—can be criticized, physicalists nonetheless feel assured that some version of physicalism must be true. This assurance may arise in part from their conviction that there is neither good evidence nor a good argument for the opposing view (the view that the mind is immaterial) and in part from their conviction that science is, slowly but surely, uncovering the physical workings of the mind. Beyond this, most physicalists—or rather, most physicalists of the non-eliminativist stripe—maintain that the truth of physicalism is strongly suggested by what has come to be known as 'the causal argument for physicalism'.

The causal argument begins with the premise that the mind can make your body move; that, for example, your feeling of thirst and your belief that there is a glass of water near you can cause you to pick up the glass and bring it to your lips. Add to this premise the claim that physiology reveals that such bodily movements are fully caused by lower-level physical processes (electrical impulses travel along nerve fibers, which innervate muscles, which move limbs) and the assumption that (although every once in a while some effect might have two distinct causes, such as when someone dies from both being struck by lightning and being shot through the heart) things are not systematically doubly caused, and we have the complete causal argument. To adopt Ryle's trope of 'the ghost in the machine', which we encountered in the previous chapter, a non-physical mind would be like a ghost in a machine that has the power to flip switches in the machine, thereby causing it to move. The causal argument asserts that since we have good reason to believe that all machine switches are flipped on or off by other physical parts of the machine and since it is absurd to think that the switches are doubly flipped by both the machine and the ghost, there is no ghost in the machine. Similarly, the physicalist argues, there is no non-physical mind in a physical body causing it to move since all bodily movements have physical causes, making non-physical causes redundant. Physicalism, it is concluded, must be true, even if we do not know the details of exactly how it is true.

Does the causal argument present a strong case for physicalism? Many think that it does, but, like all arguments in philosophy, it has its cracks. Some have argued that, despite appearances, the mind is merely epiphenomenal, merely a by-product of neural processes without any causal influence on the body. The machine produces the ghost, but the ghost has no effect on the machine. This 'epiphenomenalism' likens mentality to the smoke emanating from the smokestack of an old-fashioned locomotive: it is caused by, but does not propel, the body.

Others who reject physicalism think that the purported physical causes of bodily movements (and of everything else) are themselves imbued with mind. Such 'panpsychists' maintain that everything from quarks to quasars is conscious. Panpsychists can accept that all actions we undertake have bodily causes, yet they think that these bodily causes are, at a fundamental level, also mental. Some panpsychists claim to find support for their view in the idea that physics reveals only what things do and nothing of what things are; it reveals that electrons repel other electrons but not what electrons, themselves, are. It may be a bit of a leap, but some panpsychists find it natural to infuse what physics leaves open with consciousness.

Panpsychism is generally seen as contrary to physicalism since it posits that consciousness is a fundamental feature of the world, not built up out of physical parts. Yet since panpsychists generally maintain consciousness is an aspect of all the fundamental particles and forces of physics, panpsychism also, in a sense, accounts for mind in terms of the fundamental particles of physics. This feature of panpsychism leads some to categorize it as a version of physicalism even though, to return to the Rylian analogy, the panpsychist believes that the machine is composed of parts, all of which have a touch of the ghost.

Non-reductive physicalism and emergentism

Although not many dualists uphold the belt and braces account of mind according to which our bodily actions are doubly caused by physical bodily processes and non-physical mental processes, non-reductive physicalists—physicalists who reject both the identity theory and eliminativism about the mind—accept double causation so long as the overdetermining causes are intimately connected. Non-reductive physicalists think that the mind is a higher level feature of the brain, much as a mountain is a higher level feature of the molecules it is made out of, and think that causal overdetermination is rife in nature.

Some have argued that non-reductive physicalism's acceptance of over-determination makes the theory untenable since it drains away the causal powers of the mind: if your action of reaching for a glass when you're thirsty is fully caused by neurophysiological processes, your thirst (which on the non-reductive account is not reducible to neurophysiological processes) would seem to have nothing to do with it. Given that central to our conception of human action is the idea that our beliefs and desires are a causal force of our actions, any theory of the mind that fails to account for the causal powers of the mind would seem to be in serious trouble.

Non-reductive physicalists, however, don't think lower level causation excludes higher level causation. Think of how burning gasoline causes parts of your car's engine to move. The gasoline that fuels your car is made from (is a higher-level feature of) various hydrocarbons and ethanol. So it seems that the hydrocarbons and ethanol also cause your car to move. Moreover, since gasoline is multiply realizable—not only did gasoline once contain lead, the mix of hydrocarbons can change, as can the percentage of ethanol—it is not reducible to one set of chemical components: all the different mixtures still count as gasoline. According to the non-reductive physicalist, just as gasoline powers cars while hydrocarbons and ethanol are busy doing this job as well, your intention to drink a glass of water causes you to reach for a glass even while certain neurophysiological processes are causing this as well.

Any theory of the mind that maintains that the mind is physical yet does not identify mental properties with neural or other lower-level properties (that do not themselves have a touch of the ghost) falls under the rubric of non-reductive physicalism. Thus, functionalism is sometimes understood as a version of non-reductive physicalism, as is emergentism.

Emergentism dictates that the emergence of mind from brain is analogous to the emergence of the wetness of water from H_2O molecules or to the emergence of an image of a face from the colourful, patterned grid of squares in a Chuck Close portrait. In neither case is the relation between the whole and its parts additive (the mass of an object is additive inasmuch as its mass is equal to the sum of the masses of its parts but individual H_2O molecules are not wet and the squares of the Chuck Close painting are not small sections of a face). Nor is it merely synergistic (two drugs work together synergistically if their combined effect is more than the sum of the effects of the drugs taken individually).

Rather, with emergence, quantitative changes give rise to qualitative ones, or as the physicist Philip Anderson put it, 'more is different'.

All emergentists agree with Anderson's sentiment, but not all think, as the wetness/H_2O analogy might suggest, that an explanation of how consciousness emerges out of biological processes is forthcoming.

Chapter 4
Intentionality

Imagine you're spending the day at New York City's Coney
Island, watching the waves gradually wash up pieces of driftwood,
bottle caps polished pebbles, and seaweed. As the tide begins to
recede, you notice that the residue seems to form a mosaic of
Abraham Lincoln, highlighting his prominent brows, stovetop
hat, and razor-blade-sharp cheekbones. Does the debris on its
own create a picture of Lincoln? Or is it a picture of Lincoln only
because you interpret it as such?

Looking up at the cottony cumulus clouds, you spy a formation
that looks to you like your neighbour's basset hound. Does the
formation *represent* the hound? If you were at work staring at
clouds on your screen saver, would that same cottony cloud
formation at the beach still count as a floating sculpture, however
insubstantial, of your neighbour's dog?

Next day, you visit an art gallery downtown and see a bottle cap
mosaic entitled 'Honest Abe.' This time, it's clearly Lincoln. Even
3-year-old Kymani's stick figure rendition of Lincoln, you might
say (especially, if you are one of Kymani's parents), counts as a
drawing of, or representation of, Lincoln. But while Kymani and
other artists create their masterpieces deliberately, the ocean had
no such goal; it was a fluke. Is this relevant to the question of
whether the surf washed up a veritable picture of Lincoln? And

what do cumulus clouds and aleatoric arrangements of driftwood have to do with the mind anyway?

While there is disagreement among philosophers as to whether unwitnessed flotsam and jetsam could count as a representation of something, there is quite a bit of agreement about the relevance of representation to the mind. Our mental states are capable of representing things in the world; our thoughts about Lincoln *represent* him; our belief that he was the sixteenth president of the United States is a belief *about* him; and when his contemporaries saw the individual who was described during his campaign as having 'the leanest, lankiest, most ungainly mass of legs, arms and hatchet face ever strung upon a single frame', they had a visual perception *of* him. It is this property of the mind—the mind's ability to represent things in the world—that the 19th-century German philosopher Franz Brentano referred to as 'object-directedness', and what contemporary philosophers refer to as 'intentionality'. Philosophers today aim to better understand intentionality, its role in our mental lives, and the challenges it poses for a physical account of the world.

Intentionality and the direction of fit

Various kinds of mental states seem to possess 'intentionality'; they seem, in other words, to be about things, in the sense that my belief that there is an apple in the fruit bowl is *about* that apple in the bowl. The apple itself isn't about anything, but my belief is: it's about the apple. Because beliefs are about things, philosophers classify them as 'intentional states'. The terminology can be confusing since the word 'intention' has a standard meaning: to intend to do something is to plan to do it. But the word 'intentional', in the context of philosophy of mind, is a technical term. Philosophers would count your intention (in the sense of planning) to skip work and go beachcombing as one type of intentional state because your plan is about something: skipping work and going to the beach. Beliefs, desires, hopes, and fears, however, also exhibit intentionality: if you believe that you are at the beach, your belief is about the beach; if you hope that the weather cooperates, your hope is about the weather. Perceptions, according to many, also have 'aboutness' or representational content. If I see the waves, my visual experience represents those waves. When I hear the surf, I have an auditory experience of the waves breaking on the shore. All such mental states are intentional, as philosophers use this term, since all of these mental states are *about*, or in some sense *point to* things in the world.

The 20th-century English philosopher Elizabeth Anscombe divides intentional states into two groups by means of an analogy. Imagine setting off to the grocery store armed with a shopping list that reads, 'peas, carrots, potatoes, and brussels sprouts'. This list does not represent the world as it is—it doesn't identify those items that you have purchased—but is rather a representation of what you intend, or plan to put in your cart and purchase. Similarly, intentional mental states, such as desires, hopes, and intentions (in the sense of plans), represent not the way the world is, but rather the way you desire, hope, or intend it to be. The shopping list represents items that you desire to purchase, and your desire to eat a large bowl of smashed peas represents a state of the world (you eating smashed peas) that you hope will come to fruition.

Hopes and desires have what is referred to as a 'world-to-mind direction of fit'. It is the world that needs to be adjusted to fit your shopping list. And this means that mistakes on the list are rectified by changing the world, not the list. For example, if you notice upon arriving at the cash register that you forgot to purchase peas, the way to rectify this is by changing what is in your shopping cart rather than by changing the list. Similarly, it is the world that needs to give way in order to fit your desire for smashed peas: to satisfy the desire, you change the world by smashing those peas.

In contrast to hopes and desires, beliefs and perceptions aim to represent the world as it actually is; as such, beliefs and perceptions are said to have a 'mind-to-world direction of fit'. They are more like the tally that the cashier generates when you make your purchase. If the cashier double charges you for the sack of potatoes, you'd most likely take your business elsewhere if, after pointing out the error, you were told to turn your cart around and pick up another. It is the tally that wants revision, not your cart. Similarly, if upon slicing your purple majesty potatoes you learn that your belief about the colour of their flesh was mistaken, you would revise your belief and not the potatoes.

Puzzling cases of intentionality

There are four interrelated problems, or as some see them, paradoxes of intentionality. The first concerns the nature of our beliefs about things that do not exist. If I believe that my office window is open, my belief seems to be directed at the window in my office. But what makes this belief *about* the window? What gives it its intentionality? At a most basic level, my belief's ability to represent the window seems to depend on how I, the believer, am related to the window; because I see the window and see that it is open, I believe that it is open. Yet we can also have beliefs about things that do not exist. The fountain of youth does not exist, yet Ponce de León believed that it did; he had a belief *about* the fountain. There are no perpetual motion machines—machines that work indefinitely without an energy source. The laws of thermodynamics forbid them. Yet we can think about perpetual motion machines; indeed, so many people have tried to design them that the United States Patent and Trademark Office requires that proposals for perpetual motion machines, and only for such machines, include a working model (Figure 4). What is Ponce de León thinking about when he thinks about the fountain of youth? Not something in the external world, as there is no such thing. The obvious answer might seem to be: something in his mind, perhaps a mental picture of the fountain of youth. But this can't

4. A 1660 wood engraving of Robert Fludd's 1618 'water screw', a device that was designed to perpetually pump water back into its own supply tank by means of a water wheel and Archimedean screw.

be right either since he doesn't believe he may find an idea of the fountain of youth; he believes he may find the fountain of youth itself.

A second problem concerns hallucinations. It seems that from a first-person point of view, my perception of a window in my office and a hallucination of a window in my office might be indistinguishable. If some crazed philosopher were to sneak into my office overnight, plaster over the window, and slip a powerful hallucinogen into my tea, causing me to hallucinate a window that looked just like my old window, I might not notice that my office had changed. Theories of intentionality do not need to explain the motives of this crazed, drug-pushing, nocturnal philosopher, but they should, many think, be able to account for how perceptions of windows and hallucinations of windows can seem to be about the same thing.

A third problem any theory of intentionality needs to contend with is that I not only believe that my window is open right now but also that office windows make people more productive. In this case, I don't have a belief about any particular window. Instead, I have a belief about office windows in general. Similarly, I may want a cat even if there is no one particular cat that I have in mind that I want. What is the intentional object of my desire for a cat? Do we need to account for two different forms of intentionality, one that is directed at actual machines, particular cats, and office windows, and another that is directed at hallucinations, general things such as cats, and non-things such as perpetual motion machines? Philosophers tend to favour unity and so are disinclined to divide and conquer.

Finally, a fourth problem concerns the way in which we seem to believe things only under a certain description. For example, consider Claudia. Claudia believes that the Parthenon is in Greece. Yet even though 'Hellas' is just another name for Greece, if you were to ask her, 'is the Parthenon in Hellas?', she'd say, 'no, it's in Greece'. Thus, it might seem that she does not believe that the Parthenon is in Hellas. However, if intentionality depends on the relation between believers and objects believed, then, since Hellas is one and the same object as Greece, it seems that she should also believe that the Parthenon is in Hellas.

Intentionality as the mark of the mental

Many of our mental states are representational, but are all mental states representational? Brentano thought that they were. Beliefs, desires, hopes, fears, doubts, suspicions, loves, and lusts all point to things in the world. The defining feature of the mind, or the 'mark of the mental', is, according to Brentano, intentionality. As such, he held that not only do all components of the mind exhibit intentionality, but all things that exhibit intentionality are components of the mind.

Ascertaining the mark of the mental has sometimes been thought of as the first step in a philosophical investigation of the mind, the idea being that in order to investigate something you need to know what it is that you are aiming to investigate. Of course, to a large degree, definitions and investigations advance together. And, in particular, although studying the mind requires some starting point, or provisional understanding of what you are setting out to study, a complete definition, or rather increasingly better definitions, only arises after some studying takes place. If there is a reciprocal relationship between definitions and enquiry—with enquiry leading to better definitions, which lead to further and better enquiry, which leads to still further and better definition and so on—mark-hunting at the outset of enquiry might be pointless.

Reciprocity, however, takes time. And philosophers, though they have been known to plug away at a single problem till the grave, are sometimes impatient. Besides, many seem to plainly enjoy defining things, especially when this involves identifying necessary and sufficient conditions for the concept in question. One can think of it as a game (with the project of finding necessary and sufficient conditions for what it is to be a game, being one much-discussed move in this game). The rules are simple: the first player suggests that p is a necessary and sufficient condition for q and the second player (or perhaps an entire team) tries to show that either p is not necessary for q or that it is not sufficient for it or, for the most points, that it is neither necessary nor sufficient for q. Brentano has already made the first move in proposing that intentionality is necessary and sufficient for mentality. Let's play.

Is intentionality necessary for mentality? That is to say, do all mental states exhibit intentionality? Brentano's student the German phenomenologist Edmund Husserl defended Brentano's view; according to Husserl, 'consciousness is always consciousness of an object'. If you think about the mouse behind the wainscot, your thought is directed at the mouse. When the little creature scampers across the room and into the kitchen, you will, if you are observant, have a visual perception of the mouse. You may also believe that the poor thing is more afraid of you than you are of it. Your thoughts, perceptions, and beliefs about the mouse all seem to be intentional conscious states.

However, as both Brentano and Husserl recognize, there are at least apparent counterexamples to the view that all mental states exhibit intentionality. Although beliefs, desires, perceptions, and many other mental states may be object directed, certain sensations and moods don't seem to point to anything. For example, some have argued that bodily pain, though unpleasant, is not representational. Or consider sadness. Often, when you're feeling blue, you're sad about something. But, arguably, sometimes one just feels sad. The same goes for free-floating anxiety. Although one may be anxious about global warming, it might be that one could experience anxiety without being anxious about anything. While some philosophers see such experiences as counterexamples to the view that all mental states are intentional, others do not. Pain, they will say, represents the location in the body where the pain is occurring, and undirected sadness or free-floating anxiety are directed at events that you don't want to explicitly recognize. This round in the defining game ends in a tie; let's go to the next.

How does intentionality fare as a sufficient condition for mentality? If something exhibits intentionality, is it perforce mental? It might seem that the answer to this question is clearly 'no'. Melville's novel *Moby-Dick* is about Ishmael's recounting of Ahab's monomaniacal hunt for a great white whale; Da Vinci's *Mona Lisa* represents a half-smiling woman; and the New York City subway map is a map of the largest subway system (in terms of number of stations) on the planet. Yet, although novels, paintings, maps, sentences, and signs are about things, they are, some argue, only about things inasmuch as we take them to be about things: a stop sign has no meaning in and of itself but means stop—it is *about* stopping—only because we interpret it to mean this.

The distinction between a thought having intentionality in and of itself and a sign having intentionality in virtue of how we interpret it is referred to as the distinction between 'intrinsic' or 'original intentionality' and 'derived intentionality'. Original intentionality is understood as intentionality that can exist even if no one else is there to witness it. Your beliefs and thoughts about the novel *Moby-Dick* are said to have original intentionality. No one else needs to interpret them as being about the novel to make them about the novel; thus, they have intentionality in and of themselves. In contrast, the novel *Moby-Dick* is derivatively intentional; it is about Ahab's quest only because it was created to or interpreted as such by us.

Of course, the novel is about so much more than Ahab's quest, and it is worth pondering the relation between authorial intent and reader's interpretation. These are topics best left to other books in the *Very Short Introduction* series. What matters to philosophers of mind about novels is that they can be about something at all and that their being about something seems to depend not only on the words in them but also on the minds that interpret or create them. The same goes for paintings, maps, street signs, and aleatoric arrangements of driftwood that we see as representing Lincoln. If intrinsic intentionality belongs exclusively to the mind, then being intrinsically intentional would seem to be sufficient for mentality. And if so, round two is a win for Brentano.

Of course, there are very few winning moves in the game of finding necessary and sufficient conditions. Perhaps, one might argue, a robot could have intrinsically intentional states yet not have a mind. If things without minds can be intrinsically intentional, then a physicalistic account of intentionality would seem to be within reach. But if intentionality cannot be accounted for in entirely physical terms, the mind would not fit into the physical world and physicalism would therefore be false.

Is intentionality physical?

Consider the following argument: (1) minds have intentionality; (2) nothing physical has intentionality; therefore (3) minds cannot be physical. The argument is, as philosophers put it, 'valid': if the premises of a valid argument are true, then the conclusion of the argument must be true as well. Thus, if the premises of this argument against physicalism are true—if it is true that minds exhibit intentionality and that nothing physical does—then it must be true that minds are not physical; if the premises of this argument are true, we would have irrefutable proof that the mind is immaterial. But are the premises true? In other words—again, philosopher's words—is the argument sound? (A sound argument is both valid and contains all true premises.)

Let us assume that we have beliefs and desires and that these beliefs and desires have intentionality. The key issue then becomes whether no physical things exhibit intentionality, or, more specifically, whether no physical things exhibit intrinsic intentionality. Of course, if the mind is a physical thing, then there are physical things that exhibit intrinsic intentionality. But let us leave open the question of whether the mind is physical and ask whether any physical things (apart from the potential exception of the mind) have intentionality. (What counts as a physical thing? Although this is a topic of debate, here we can understand the claim that the mind is physical to mean that the mind is ultimately reducible to or built out of parts that are not themselves mental.)

Circling back to our initial example, does the debris on the beach (which is a scattering of physical objects) in and of itself represent Lincoln? I think most of us would say that it doesn't, that it represents Lincoln only because we interpret it to do so. Similarly, the table I'm writing at is neither about a table nor about my writing; rather, it's just a table, and the electrochemical activity conducted by the mass of neurons in my brain while I'm thinking about the table seems (in terms of its intentionality) no different. True enough, we speak as if neurons communicate across synapses by sending signals, yet such 'communication' is, most would say, no more intentional than the signal created by a change in voltage in an electrical cable. In other words, it seems that the neural structures that underlie my thoughts and beliefs about things are, themselves, not about anything either. Rather, they seem to be just physical bits of matter, which, like any other physical bits of matter, don't intrinsically represent anything.

The 20th-century American philosopher Jerry Fodor, putting his point in a deliberately paradoxical way, maintained that 'if [intentionality] is real, it must really be something else'. What he, meant by this was that if intentionality exists—if our beliefs and desires can really be *about* things—then intentionality must be explainable in terms of things which may give rise to intentionality but do not have intrinsic intentionality themselves. The project of explaining intentionality in terms of ordinary physical objects, that is, explaining it without invoking the concept of intentionality itself—explaining it non-circularly—is referred to as 'naturalizing' intentionality. If intentionality can be naturalized, then the mind's ability to represent objects in the world will no longer prevent us from thinking about the mind as a physical object.

The pictorial account of representation

Philosophical problems are supposed to be difficult. But is the project of naturalizing intentionality so daunting? Perhaps physical objects can represent things simply through the relation of pictorial resemblance: pictures of Lincoln—whether drawn by a human or washed up on the beach—represent Lincoln because they resemble Lincoln. Moreover, if, as the 17th-century English philosopher John Locke maintained, ideas are 'the pictures drawn in our minds', the explanation for how mental states acquire intentionality is that they are pictorial, that when I think about an apple, I picture an apple in my mind and that my thought is about an apple because the picture in my mind represents an apple. Simple, right?

Although this pictorial account may be simple to state, many have thought it is not at all simple to make sense of; indeed, according to the 20th-century American philosopher Nelson Goodman, 'more error could hardly be compressed into so short a formula'. One problem with the pictorial account of intentionality is that not all thoughts, hopes, and beliefs have images associated with them. For example, my hope for world peace is not connected to a picture of world peace. And it is not clear how a pictorial account of intentionality can explain the thoughts, hopes and beliefs of those with aphantasia, a condition that, while apparently having no impact on creative thought, makes voluntary mental imagery impossible. Such considerations suggest that pictorial resemblance is not necessary for intentionality.

Is pictorial resemblance sufficient for intentionality? Goodman argues that pictures are more forgiving than intentional states. A picture of Albert Einstein resembles Einstein, but it also resembles Walter Matthau who played Einstein in the 1994 romantic comedy *I.Q.* Yet thoughts about Einstein are thoughts about him and not Matthau. Indeed, a physical picture of Einstein—which is flat, rectangular, and relatively easy to pick up—seems, in many ways, to resemble any other picture, be it of Einstein, Matthau, or the Eiffel Tower (all of which are flat, rectangular, and easy to pick up), more than it resembles any person. Furthermore, images are ambiguous in a way that thoughts are not. As Wittgenstein pointed out, a drawing of a person walking uphill may be indistinguishable from a drawing of a person sliding downhill backwards (Figure 5). However, your thought about a person walking uphill is not ambiguous in this way.

More generally, resemblance is typically understood as an 'equivalence relation', meaning that it is reflexive (everything

5. 'I see a picture; it represents an old man walking up a steep path leaning on a stick.—How? Might it not have looked just the same if he had been sliding downhill in that position? Perhaps a Martian would describe the picture so.' (Ludwig Wittgenstein, Part 1, *Philosophical Investigations*.)

resembles itself), symmetric (if A resembles B, then B resembles A), and transitive (if A resembles B and B resembles C, then A resembles C), whereas intentionality is not an equivalence relation: it's not the case that everything is about itself, and it is not the case that if my thought is about a cup, then the cup is about my thought, and it's not the case if you think about my thoughts about a cup, you're necessarily thinking about the cup.

Perhaps you are beginning to appreciate Goodman's comment about the density of errors in the idea that intentionality is reducible to resemblance.

The causal account of intentionality

Unsurprisingly, the resemblance account of intentionality has few adherents. A more promising account, many think, is the idea that intentionality arises when two events or objects co-vary with each other. Tree rings co-vary with the age of a tree: the more rings, the older the tree. On this account of intentionality, tree rings, therefore, *represent* a tree's age. Unlike words on a page or clouds in the sky that represent things only inasmuch as we understand them as doing so, it is argued that tree rings are a 'natural sign' of a tree's age; they represent a tree's age regardless of whether anyone interprets them as doing so; they have intrinsic intentionality. Similarly, a shadow that is cast towards the east is seen as a natural sign of the sun being in the west.

What underlies these natural signs, it is thought, is the systematic causal connections between the sign, on the one hand, and what the sign represents, on the other. The change in seasons (on planet Earth) that coincides with the passing of years causes the rings in a tree trunk, and the position of the sun in the west causes a shadow to be cast towards the east. If intentionality can arise in trees and shadows, the argument that minds cannot be physical because minds have intentionality and nothing physical can have intentionality, though valid, is not sound because the premise 'nothing physical has intentionality' is false.

Of course, the mere correlation between two events might not suffice for the one event to represent or be about the other. Imagine that during a two-minute period, your heartbeat correlated perfectly with the heartbeat of your cousin Imani's? This correlation, it seems, could be a fluke and could exist without your heartbeat representing Imani's heartbeat. If so, mere correlation is insufficient for representation. However, the relation between the rings of the tree and the age of a tree is not one of mere correlation; rather, the relation is a correlation brought about as a result of causation. The same might be said of the relation between the electrochemical activity in your visual cortex when you have a perception of a tree and the tree itself: it's causal. Does correlation brought about by causation suffice for representation?

Let us say you live in Nepal and regularly see and admire a mountain that you think is Mt Everest. But it's not Mt Everest; it's Mt Kangchenjunga. Your thought that Mt Everest is sublime misrepresents Mt Kangchenjunga as Mt Everest, yet according to the causal account of intentionality, since your thought is caused by Mt Kangchenjunga, it should be about Mt Kangchenjunga. Of course, the correlation between your admiration of what you take to be Mt. Everest and your visual experiences of Mt Kanchenjunga is not as tight as the correlation between tree rings and the age of trees. Someone could have corrected you and you would have no longer been mistaken.

But let us thicken the plot: imagine that, unbeknownst to you, you are part of an experiment on mind manipulation. Lab technicians have hooked your brain up to receive computer-generated electrical input that causes you to think about Mt Everest. If you were in this situation, your thoughts of Mt Everest would be invariably caused, not by Mt Everest, but by certain computer-generated electrical impulses to your brain. On the causal account, your thoughts and perceptions would then, it seems, represent the impulses. Yet this doesn't seem right.

Returning to those pesky non-existent objects, one might also ask how the causal account can explain a child's belief in Santa Claus. Two-year-old Paco believes in Santa Claus, yet Santa Claus does not cause his belief. Even if one wants to say that there is a causal chain that reaches from Paco back to the 4th-century Greek Christian bishop Saint Nicholas of Myra, who gave gifts to the poor, Paco's belief is not about this bishop. Could Paco's belief be caused by (and therefore about) about the concept of Santa Claus? The concept exists. But, in line with what we found when considering the

Fountain of Youth, if 'Santa Claus' refers to the concept of Santa Claus, then Paco's belief that Santa Claus exists is true.

Finally, one might wonder where the causal chain is supposed to begin. On the causal account of intentionality, when you see a mountain—when you have a perception *of* the mountain—your visual perception is caused by the mountain: light is reflected off the mountains, then enters your eye. Yet, why say that you are perceiving the mountain rather than perceiving the light? The light is also causing you to have a visual image of the mountain. Or why do we not say that we are seeing the sun since the sun caused the light that reflected off the mountain? If the computer programmer who created the code that caused you to think about Mt. Everest had a perception of the mountain that was caused by the mountain, should we say that in the lab your thoughts about Mt. Everest *are* caused by the mountain? Indeed, why on a causal account of intentionality aren't all perceptions really perceptions of the ultimate cause of everything: the big bang? A causal account of intentionality needs to be able to respond to these questions.

The teleological account of intentionality

The function of our sweat is to cool our bodies; the function of a plant's xylem is to transport water and nutrients; the function of the protective protein coat of a virus is to protect the virus while it enters a host. Teleology is the study of functions, or purposes, and the teleological account of intentionality aims to naturalize intentionality by explaining it in terms of functions, sometimes specifically biological functions: in our evolutionary history, since interpreting the sounds that our conspecifics make as warning of giant hyenas or saber-toothed cats was advantageous, as was producing such sounds, those sounds developed the function of warning others of predators, thereby making such warnings—and by extension our thoughts about such warnings—about the predators.

The contemporary American philosopher Ruth Millikan illustrates how the function of an action can bestow it with intentionality by leveraging two non-human animal actions. Beavers, as she explains, thwack the water with their tails to alert other beavers of danger. Because both making the thwack at a propitious time and interpreting it as a warning were advantageous, they evolved in tandem, with the thwack developing the function of representing danger. Honeybees rapidly wag their abdomens as they trace and retrace a pattern in the hive—performing what is called a "waggle dance"—to indicate the direction of and distance to a bountiful source of nectar. By functioning as a set of directions for the other bees in the hive, the waggle dance comes to represent the location of and distance to food.

With this bare-bones account of teleosemantics in place, we are ready to examine the opponent's favourite objection: swamp creatures! Imagine that lightning strikes a swamp and that, against all odds, as the charge ignites the partially decomposed plant matter and water-saturated soil it brings into existence a fully formed, conscious human being, complete with what would seem to be beliefs about the past and desires for the future, including, for example, the desire to leave the swamp and put on some dry clothes. The question is, what ought a proponent of a teleological account of intentionality say about the swamp creature's (purported) thoughts? The swamp creature lacks the evolutionary history that, on the teleological account, breathes intentionality into brain processes. Must proponents of biosemantics reject the idea that this swamp creature could have beliefs and desires about things? The issue is unresolved.

To show how the mind fits into the physical world, we need a physical account of intentionality. Yet naturalizing intentionality, it turns out, is no easy matter, perhaps especially if, as some think, to explain intentionality, we need to invoke the idea that belief states are conscious or at least capable of being conscious.

Chapter 5
Consciousness

The late 19th-century American psychologist and philosopher William James wrote that 'there is but one indefectibly certain truth, and that is the truth...that the present phenomenon of consciousness exists'. Yet what is consciousness? Although we may know what consciousness is by having it, once we try to put what we know into words, the certainty, James admits, dissolves. Nonetheless, a central project in philosophy of mind is finding words to explain conscious experience. What is the nature of consciousness? What purpose does it serve? Is there something about consciousness that precludes scientific scrutiny? Are we capable of being mistaken about our own conscious experiences? And, despite James's indefectible silent-certainty, could we be mistaken that consciousness exists at all?

Defining consciousness

What are we trying to understand when we try to understand consciousness? Not only do philosophers have no agreed-upon definition of consciousness, some think that it can't be defined at all, that you can understand conscious experiences only by having them. Such philosophers see consciousness as Louis Armstrong purportedly saw jazz: if you need to ask what it is, you're never going to know.

Indeed, the task of explaining consciousness to someone who professes not to know—and there are philosophers who do profess this—is much more challenging than that of explaining jazz to the uninitiated. If you don't know what jazz is, you can at least listen to music that is classified as jazz and compare it to its precursor ragtime, its cousin the blues, and its alter ego classical music. Presumably, such an exercise will give you a sense of jazz. But with consciousness, there is nothing to compare it to, since when you are not conscious, you are not aware of anything. Furthermore, jazz has been highly theorized since Armstrong's time, so a trip through the New York Public Library for the Performing Arts may very well provide some insight into the nature of jazz for those who do not know.

Nevertheless, there are written accounts of consciousness intended to provide a sense of what consciousness is for those who claim not to know. Consciousness, it is said, is the state you are in when you are awake or dreaming and what you lack when you are in a dreamless sleep, under anaesthesia, or in a coma. Yet for those who claim not to know what the word 'consciousness' means, such an explanation will fall flat. Which aspect of being awake illustrates consciousness? Without knowledge of the relevant difference between being awake and being in a dreamless sleep, it would be difficult to know. After all, when I'm awake, my brain activity is different from when I'm in a dreamless sleep, but if I had wanted to convey that consciousness is merely a certain form of brain activity, I could have done that directly. Of course, you may have understood the proffered explanation of consciousness, but I imagine that you understood what consciousness was before you read it.

What it's like

Some of the very same philosophers who think that nothing can be said to enlighten those who claim to not know what consciousness is have found quite a bit to say about what it is to those who claim to already know. And much of their discussion centres on the idea that for you to be conscious there has to be something it is like to be you: while rocks have no inner experiences—or so most presume—and thus there is nothing it is like to be a rock, you know that there is something it is like to be you, something it is like to savour your morning coffee, to feel the soft fur of a kitten, to feel the sting when that adorable kitten scratches you. These experiences are conscious experiences; they have what philosophers refer to as 'qualitative content' or 'qualia'; there is *something it is like* to have these experiences. And that there is something it is like to have the wealth of experiences we have is, according to various philosophers, what makes life worth living. To be sure, whether the meaning of life resides in inner experience or in outward actions aimed at making the world a better place is worth pondering. But in any event, it does seem that without consciousness, something significant about our lives would be missing.

The claim that to be conscious is for there to be 'something it is like to be you' can be described in terms of having a 'point of view', or a 'perspective'. To have a point of view in this sense is simply to be the locus of conscious experience. Of course, to explain consciousness in terms of having a point of view and then to explain what it is to have a point of view in terms of being conscious is circular. Yet, on the assumption that we cannot explain consciousness in terms of something else (you're not going to understand it, unless you have it), such a circle is to be expected—whether it is a virtuous or a vicious one, however, can be debated.

The American philosopher Thomas Nagel presents a thought experiment that illustrates what it means to have a point of view by highlighting how difficult it is to know what an entirely unfamiliar type of conscious experience is like. Try to imagine, he asks us, what it is like to be a bat and navigate via echolocation. Can you imagine this? The best you could do, Nagel argues, would be to imagine what it would be like, not for a bat, but for *you* to fly in the dark. Bats seem to be conscious, yet they are different enough from us, according to Nagel, that we cannot know what their experience of the world is like; even though we may be fairly certain that bats have conscious experiences, no amount of objective information can ever reveal a bat's inner life; even a virtual reality simulation that allows us to experience what it would be like to fly around in a dark cave, drink the blood of sleeping sheep, and hang upside down provides only a human's perspective what it is like to do these things. No matter how much third-person information we acquire about bats, Nagel argues, nothing allows us to understand the bat's first-person perspective. If you want to know what it's like to experience the world via echolocation, according to Nagel, you've got to experience echolocation.

Is this correct? It isn't true that no humans know what it is like to echolocate: some blind individuals rely on echolocation to get around, making clicking sounds and listening to the echoes that bounce off objects; some are so adept at it that they can identify an object's shape, distance, and material. These individuals know what it is like to use echolocation to navigate and thus would seem to have some insight into what it is like to be a bat. Such an objection, however, misses the point. It does not illustrate how one could come to understand the bat's experience of echolocation without experiencing echolocation oneself. Similar to the argument in Chapter 1 about Mary—Mary, it is claimed, cannot know what it is like to see colour without seeing colour—Nagel's point is that to understand what it is like to navigate via echolocation you need to have experienced echolocation.

Other creatures may have sensory systems that are even more foreign to us. For example, dolphins perceive electrical stimuli via electroreception and wood mice detect magnetic fields via magnetoreception. Presumably, there is something it is like for these creatures to perceive the world as they do. Yet, according to

Nagel, third-person insight into these sensory experiences falls short of first-person understanding.

Even other humans can be a mystery to us. The philosopher L. A. Paul highlights this mystery by way of 'transformative experiences', which she understands as significant, novel experiences that, no matter how much information you had about them before undergoing them, affect you in a way that is both profound and unpredictable. An example of a transformative experience is becoming a parent: if you have never been a parent, no matter how much others tell you about the joy of seeing that first smile and the despondency of chronic sleep deprivation, you will not understand these experiences until you undergo them yourself. Understanding what it is like to live in extreme poverty, Paul argues, is similarly opaque to those of us living in comparative opulence, as is the experience of someone who is transgendered to someone who is cisgendered. One could even argue that some of the experiences of your past self are opaque to your present self. For example, for those who have already gone through it once, the memory of what it was like to undergo the pain of childbirth may have receded to such a degree that it is no longer possible to understand what it was like. If so, there is a sense in which we do not even know what it is like to be ourselves.

Different forms of consciousness

Even if it is hopeless to explain consciousness non-circularly, it might not be hopeless to elucidate some of its forms. For example, although I can't be sure how alert you are right now, I do know that you are conscious. You also have conscious *experiences*: you are most likely having the conscious experience of seeing the page in front of you; or perhaps you are consciously experiencing your judgement about what is written on the page in front of you. When we speak of being conscious and of having conscious experiences, we are evoking two different notions of consciousness. The first, what the philosopher David Rosenthal dubs 'creature consciousness', is attributed to humans (and other creatures capable of being conscious), while the second, what he dubs 'state consciousness', is attributed to various mental states such as conscious perceptions, sensations, and thoughts. When we are creature conscious, our various conscious states can come and go. For example, gazing at the sky, you may have a conscious experience of, to quote Emerson, 'pink flakes modulated with tints of unspeakable softness', but after the sun sets, your conscious experience of unspeakable softness will be no more.

Conscious states (conscious perceptions, thoughts, sensations, for example) can also be contrasted with subconscious states. Perhaps you've had the experience of having the solution to a sticky problem come to you in the shower. One possible explanation for how you did this is that during your shower, while consciously focusing on lathering up, your subconscious mind was working it out. Another possible explanation is that in the shower you were thinking consciously yet effortlessly about the problem, in a way that hardly felt like thinking at all. Or perhaps you were employing peripheral conscious thought to the problem. The best way to see a faint distant object is via peripheral vision; perhaps peripheral thought might be the best way to penetrate faint ideas.

Although the idea of a creature being conscious is different from the idea of a state being conscious, some think that being conscious just is being in various conscious states. Such philosophers argue that the relation between creature consciousness and state consciousness is similar to the relation between being a colour and being red. If something is red, then it is a colour, but something can be a colour without being red. Similarly, if you have the conscious experience of seeing red, then you are conscious, but if you are conscious, you need not have the conscious experience of seeing red. It's uncontroversial that having a conscious experience requires one to be conscious and that being conscious doesn't require one to have, say, the specific conscious experience of seeing red. However, can someone ever be conscious (creature conscious) without having any conscious experiences? I leave this question for you to ponder.

Another distinction concerns the kinds of things you consciously experience. The 20th-century American philosopher Fred Dretske divides this terrain into things (such as the Empire State Building) and facts (such as the fact that the Empire State Building is tall. And the critical question here is whether we are ever conscious of things (if we are ever 'thing-aware') without being conscious of any facts about them (without being 'fact-aware').

Look at the array of spots in Figure 6(a), just long enough to see every spot.

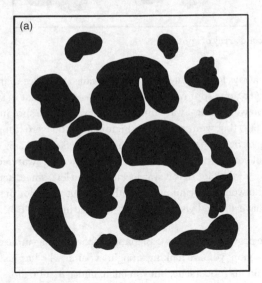

(a)

6a. First array of spots.

Now flip the page and look at the array of spots in Figure 6(b). Do the arrays look different?

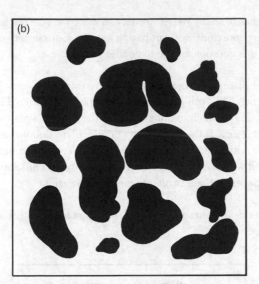

6b. Second array of spots.

Do the arrays look different? If not, you failed to notice that on Figure 6(b), one spot was removed. Dretske argues that in such a case, you were thing-aware but not fact-aware of the spot in Figure 6(a) that went missing in Figure 6(b). You were thing-aware of it because when you scanned Figure 6(a), you saw every spot, but you were not fact-aware of it (you weren't aware, for example, of the fact that it was located on the left) since, had you been, you would have known something about that spot that would have allowed you to notice its absence in Figure 6(b).

Dretske provides a similar explanation of the missing-moustache phenomenon: you are looking straight at Samir who has just shaved off his moustache, but you fail to notice that he did. You've seen Samir every day at work; thus, you were aware of his moustache. However, given that you failed to notice its absence, Dretske argues, you had not been fact-aware of the moustache.

Not everyone is convinced that Dretske's examples illustrate a distinction between fact-consciousness and thing-consciousness. Since some time elapsed from when you last saw Samir, perhaps you merely forgot that the newly whiskerless Samir had previously been mustachioed. And, although not much time elapsed between seeing Figure 6(a) and Figure 6(b), it still seems possible that your memory of that errant spot degraded rapidly. If so, you may have been fact-conscious of what you later forgot.

Ned Block argues for yet further categories of conscious experience: 'phenomenal consciousness' (p-consciousness) and 'access consciousness' (a-consciousness). Phenomenal consciousness is what Nagel's bat example is thought to elucidate. It's the type of consciousness for which there is something it is like to be conscious. When you ease into the bracing waters of Bodega Bay, there is something it is like for you to feel cold; when you stroll the summer afternoon streets of Kuwait, there is something it is like for you to experience blistering heat. Those states are p-conscious. In contrast, access consciousness generally allows you to report on and reason about your conscious states. Normally, the two go together: when you are phenomenally conscious of the summer heat, you can complain about it. But do a-consciousness and p-consciousness ever part ways?

It is not clear that there can be a-conscious states without p-conscious states. After all, if you are able to report that you are cold, it would seem that you have a feeling of coldness. But some think that p-consciousness can exist without a-consciousness. It has been argued that the tip-of-the-tongue phenomenon—'I know what that brown, fuzzy, ovoid fruit is called, but I can't bring it to mind'—is an example of being p-conscious of the word 'kiwi', but not access conscious of it. Dreaming has been suggested as another example. There seems to be something it is like to dream, but we often can't report our dreams. Moreover, there is the phenomenon of coming to notice a noise that has been present in the background for some time. Perhaps you were engaged in a conversation in earshot of a power drill. You may be so caught up in the conversation that you fail to notice the drill. In such a situation, it might be claimed, you are phenomenally conscious of the drill, but not access conscious of it. The wounded soldier in battle might be in a similar state: p-, but not a-conscious of pain.

While some argue that dissociations such as these support the idea that conscious experiences can be of the phenomenal or access variety, others are not convinced. Can you really not access what's on the tip of your tongue? If you know it's there, don't you have some access to it? For example, you might know that the name of the brown, fuzzy fruit starts with 'k'. Dreamers can sometimes alter the course of their dreams, which might suggest that they have access to their dreams while they are having them, and, of course, we sometimes do remember our dreams and can use what we remember to make decisions. On the basis of a recalled dream, you decide to stop reading horror stories right before bed. And as for unnoticed background noise and unnoticed pain, perhaps we do not have conscious experiences of these things at all.

A science of consciousness

Can there be a science of consciousness? It might be thought that a science of consciousness is impossible because consciousness is subjective and scientific enquiry is objective. Yet science is objective in the sense that it strives for objectivity in its methodology: scientists aim to cast away personal biases when they interpret data and to arrive at theories that garner complete or at least widespread agreement. Consciousness, however, is *ontologically* subjective: its existence depends on the conscious mind, on a first-person point of view. And an objective methodology may be employed to study subjective phenomena.

Perhaps, one might think, a science of consciousness is impossible because scientific insight depends on the process of observation—the data upon which theories are based are amassed after many observations—yet consciousness can't be observed. However, you can observe your own conscious experience. And if consciousness just is a neural process, consciousness may be observed in the same way neural processes are observed. Besides, many scientific theories concern unobservables. Although we can observe the effects of gravitation—we observe that the planets orbit the sun and that apples drop from trees—we do not observe gravity itself. We accept that gravity exists in order to account for such observations. Consciousness too, some argue, could be a posit that accounts for what we take to be the observable effects of being conscious.

Not only is there a possibility of a science of consciousness, but there *is* a science of consciousness; for scientists do in fact investigate subjective processes. Would you feel a bee's wing drop onto your cheek from one centimetre away? How many hairs on the back of your hand need be touched in order for you to notice that they are being touched? These are some of the many questions about conscious experiences that science has cracked (the answers are 'yes', and 'two or three'). There are also questions that scientists are aiming to crack, such as the question of how long it takes for someone to become visually conscious of a stimulus. Though there is some controversy over how to set up experiments investigating this, experiments are conducted and the results have sparked the interest of philosophers and others who are keen to find out whether tennis players have time to become conscious of the ball before they return a fast serve.

Scientists also investigate the causes and effects of pain, the role of conscious attention in action, the effect of meditation on attention, and visual, auditory and olfactory perception, to name just a few of the ontologically subjective features of the world that yield to scientific investigation. Beyond this, some neuroscientists employ functional magnetic resonance imaging to measure brain activity in order to probe the 'neural correlates of consciousness'. The neural correlates of a conscious perception of an apple, for example, are those parts of the brain that are more active when we consciously perceive the apple and less active when our perception of it is unconscious. And scientists have found that intracranial electrical stimulation of various areas in the prefrontal cortex can produce feelings of anxiety, olfactory and gustatory sensations, the urge to move and laugh, and other conscious experiences.

Furthermore, there are theories of consciousness that, though highly speculative, are produced by scientists, such as the psychologist Bernard Baars's Global Workspace and the neuroscientist Giulio Tononi's Integrated Information theory.

Thus, there is a science of consciousness.

The hard problem

But can science uncover the 'what it is like' of conscious experience? Some have argued that current scientific theories of consciousness investigate only the causes and effects of conscious experience: what your brain does when you are conscious, and how you act during certain conscious experiences, for example. And causes and effects of conscious experience are not the same thing as conscious experience. What we really want to understand is the nature of consciousness. This is the 'hard problem', as David Chalmers puts it, and it is much more difficult to crack.

The 'hard problem' arises, Chalmers argues, because science characterizes the world 'structurally', by which he means that it characterizes the world in terms of what things do but not in terms of what things are. As I mentioned in Chapter 3, physics is sometimes thought to reveal only how things behave: we learn that a body with greater mass has more inertia and that the mass of a body does not vary with changes in gravity, that light behaves both as a particle and as a wave and slows down as it passes through the air. Yet we do not learn what mass or light is apart from a set of behaviours. From physics we learn that opposite charges attract, like charges repel, and that the net charge of any isolated system never varies, but we do not learn what charge is in itself. Somewhat like a structural drawing of a building detailing how the building is to be constructed without the notes that specify what materials are to be used, the structural description of the world set forth by physics leaves open the material, or intrinsic nature of, what it describes. Consciousness, Chalmers argues, is not a structural feature of the world; thus science can never probe its 'intrinsic nature'; it can only reveal what consciousness does and not what it is like to be conscious.

You can think of the hard problem like this: it seems that even if we were to discover, as was once proposed by Francis Crick and Christof Koch, that conscious experiences occur when and only when there are 35–73 hertz oscillations in the cerebral cortex, we would still be left with the question of why these oscillations (rather than some others) produce conscious experience; we would still be left wondering how conscious experience emerges from soggy grey matter.

Not all philosophers think that the hard problem is that much harder than the so-called easy problems, and some think that solving the easy problems—identifying the neural correlates of consciousness, developing better theories of attention, memory, perception—will amount to solving the hard problem. Once we have the details worked out, the big problem will go away. In contrast, Chalmers thinks that the hard problem would remain. This doesn't mean, he explains, that there could be no science of copiousness. There could be, he thinks, but it would not provide a reductive explanation of consciousness. Rather, a science of consciousness would need to posit consciousness as a fundamental feature of the world. And if consciousness is fundamental, he argues, we should expect it, like other fundamental features of the world—mass, charge, spin—to be pervasive; we should expect to find it not only in humans and not only in all sentient creatures, but also in simpler life forms, such as plants, and even in inanimate objects. Though this position, which is a form of panpsychism, may seem absurd, Chalmers argues that it is less absurd than the idea that consciousness could be explained structurally.

The function of consciousness

What is the purpose of consciousness? Philosophers of mind think about the function of consciousness not only because the topic is intrinsically interesting, but also because it is relevant to the mind–body problem, for if consciousness has no function, the radical view that consciousness does not exist, some argue, garners support. If everything we do could be done just as well if we were not conscious, why think that we are conscious to begin with?

One natural answer to the question 'what is the purpose of consciousness' is that consciousness guides action and serves as a workspace for reasoning. When you need to decide what to wear in the morning, you consciously consider the weather. When performing a mathematical calculation, you consciously consider your calculations, and before an important conversation, you may consciously rehearse what you need to say. It also is natural to say that conscious experience motivates you: the conscious experience of an overstretched muscle might motivate you to adjust your yoga pose; the conscious experience of eating a chocolate bar might motivate you to buy another.

All this seems obvious, yet—as I'm sure you know by now—the apparent obviousness of a view rarely prevents philosophers from arguing against it, and some philosophers think that consciousness, despite appearances, is epiphenomenal (it has no purpose). Epiphenomenalists point out that we seem to be able to perform many things without conscious attention: a long-distance truck driver can seemingly drive competently without any conscious awareness of the road; people with 'blindsight'—a visual deficit rendering individuals effectively blind in part of their visual field—may correctly shape their hands when asked to reach for an object in their blind field; and athletes sometimes respond to visual cues in less time than it takes for conscious awareness of those cues to kick in. Furthermore, they argue that unconscious, rather than conscious, motivations are the driving force in life.

Such purported examples of actions that are guided unconsciously, however, have been questioned. Are long-distance truck drivers ever truly not conscious of the road? Perhaps they are conscious of their driving but then quickly forget what they were conscious of? Do people with blindsight have a deficit in their conscious perception or merely in their ability to report conscious perception? Harking back to the discussion of a-consciousness versus p-consciousness, could they be merely p-conscious of the visual stimuli in their blind field? Just how long it takes to become conscious of something is an open question, so it is also an open question whether athletes ever are in situations where they need to act before consciously registering an input. And perhaps purported unconscious desires are better understood as conscious desires that one doesn't like to admit one has. Moreover, such examples, it seems, could at best show that consciousness is epiphenomenal in certain situations.

If consciousness has no function, one might wonderer how it evolved. We do not know when it evolved and some think that, in fact, it didn't, that consciousness is instead what the evolutionary biologists Stephen Jay Gould and Richard Lewontin call a 'spandrel', a byproduct of other traits that confer a selective advantage. Gould and Lewontin borrow the term from architecture, where it refers to the two roughly triangular spaces that remain on each side of the top of an arch bounded by a rectangular wall. Just as creating spandrels is not the aim, but rather a necessary result of arch construction, consciousness, some think, was not selected for by evolution but is the result of neurological traits that were.

To be sure, biological traits that were not directly selected for can, through 'exaptation', come to serve a useful purpose, and, indeed, artistically designed architectural spandrels may offer aesthetic pleasure and religious inspiration. Yet those who think that consciousness has no function see it as conferring no benefit at all. If that idea inspires an emotional reaction in you, turn the page.

Chapter 6
Emotions

Imagine that you are in bed in that hypnagogic state between slumber and wakefulness when you hear the creak, creak of the stairs leading to your bedroom. Your heart pounds as you jolt into hyper-alertness. Who could it be? You rise to fasten the lock, but it's too late. The door swings open and Pineapple, your golden retriever, bounds onto your bed. Relieved, your blood pressure lowers and you leash her up for her walk.

How should we understand the emotional upheaval you just underwent? In answering this question, one may attempt to discern why you heard your dog's familiar paw-steps as those of an intruder. Yet questions about why one has an emotional reaction to a specific stimulus are more squarely in the domain of psychiatry than philosophy. Philosophers—in their work as philosophers, at least—are concerned with more general features of sentient creatures. And, when it comes to understanding emotions, one question philosophers of mind investigate is that most general question of all: what is an emotion? What is it about an experience that makes it an experience of an emotion?

Some emotions seem more complex than others: jealousy or *Schadenfreude* may have more layers to unearth than joy. And some people—your friends that call you up at midnight to talk for hours about their feelings—are what we call 'emotionally complicated'. But philosophers can find complexity in the simplest of things, and joy is no exception.

What happens when you feel joy? Most would say that you have a conscious experience of joy and also undergo bodily changes: your face lights up. Joy is also typically a response to something: perhaps you are joyful about being reunited with your partner after a long separation. Joy might have characteristic behaviours: when happy, you might be motivated to greet strangers on the street with a 'good morning'. Fear also has components. In our imagined scenario, in addition to the raw feeling of fear, you also had both a physiological reaction (your heart raced) and a behavioural reaction (you jumped up to lock the door); additionally, you made a judgement about what was happening (someone was walking up the stairs) and were in a certain mental state (high alert). And these processes call for explanation as well.

Should we think of emotions as necessarily encompassing all these bodily and psychological processes? Or might some be essential to the feeling, even defining what the emotion is, while others are merely along for the ride? The contemporary American philosopher Jesse Prinz dubs the problem of identifying the components of an emotion 'the problem of parts'. Although there are philosophers who identify emotions with the entire narrative, most zoom in on certain features of the narrative, features they understand as primary, with the central divide being between those who understand emotions as bodily sensations and those who understand them as judgements.

Body-based theories of emotion

William James was a proponent of the body-based theory of emotion. For James, although emotions may be caused by certain beliefs—for example, your belief that there was someone on the stairs—and although emotions may cause you to make judgements—that the imminent danger warranted action—such beliefs and judgements are not part of emotions. Rather, according to James, an emotion is the awareness of certain bodily processes; your fear is your awareness of your pounding heart, clammy hands, and tense muscles, which are all bodily responses to what you perceived as measured footsteps approaching your bedroom door.

The Danish physician Carl Lange, one of James's contemporaries, independently arrived at a similar idea, so similar that one frequently finds in the philosophical and psychological literature on emotion references to the James–Lange theory of emotion. Yet Lange went further, arguing that the emotions are the bodily changes themselves. Thus, according to Lange, your fear just is your pounding heart and clammy hands.

James's view, in contrast to Lange's, is that emotions are not the bodily perturbations themselves, but rather the experience of such perturbations, and, while not as radical, nonetheless reverses what we naturally think of as the causal order of emotions and bodily states. According to James, 'we feel sorry because we cry, angry because we strike, afraid because we tremble'. James's view, thus, implies that rather than fear causing your heart to go on overdrive, your rapidly beating heart causes your fear (see Figure 7).

The same causal connection applies to other emotions: sadness, for example, is not the cause of a bodily response to the news of a tragic event but is rather an awareness of certain bodily responses to this news. We don't cry and become lethargic because we feel sad; rather, our sadness is an awareness of the bodily sensations that accompany crying and lethargy. When in Melville's Moby-Dick, Ishmael finds himself 'growing grim about the mouth', our protagonist's feeling, on James's view, is literally an awareness, or consciousness of the downward tension in his oral commissures.

Contemporary philosophers who uphold body-based accounts of emotions think that if not James's exact account, then at least

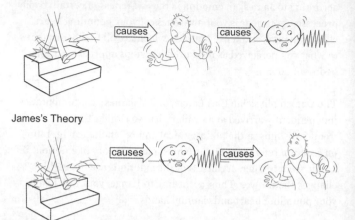

Common Sense

James's Theory

7. **Common sense and James's conception of emotion.**

something close to it is correct. They point out that there are robust correlations between bodily states and emotions. When you're afraid, your heart races; when you're embarrassed, you blush; when you're sad, you cry. Moreover, substances that change our bodily sensations can alter emotions as well. Alcohol can change one's emotion, and there is some indication that taking a pain reliever, such as acetaminophen, can alleviate not only bodily aches but also the feelings associated with romantic rejection, slights, and ostracism. One possible explanation for why acetaminophen has this effect is that experiencing such emotions simply is being aware of the relevant bodily sensations; dull the sensation and you've dulled the emotion. Furthermore, proponents of body-based theories point out that the idea of 'fake it till you make it' works with emotions: curling your lips into a smile when you're unhappy does make you feel better.

Body-based theories of emotions also reap support from practices such as yoga or meditation that emphasize how calming one's breathing is conducive to reducing anxiety. If emotions just are the awareness of bodily states, then modulating bodily states would modulate emotions.

James thought that the best evidence for his view would come from studies of people who had lost sensation in their bodies, as might happen in cases of severe spinal cord injury. If such sensory loss correlated with minimized emotional response, this would suggest that awareness of one's bodily states is essential to emotion.

How strong are these lines of support for the body-based account of emotions? The empirical data on how spinal cord injury affects one's emotions is indeterminate, and even if the data clearly indicated that quadriplegics had diminished affect, there would still be a question of how to interpret these results. Are their diminished emotional responses due to a lack of bodily awareness or could they be due to something else, such as the social isolation some quadriplegics might experience? Or let's say that quadriplegics show no sign of reduced affect. Is this because the body is not essential to emotion or is it that facial awareness alone suffices to produce emotion?

The study involving acetaminophen is open to other interpretations as well. Perhaps acetaminophen alleviates emotional pain because it alleviates the physical pain that causes emotional pain. A bout of depression, if this were the case, could be *caused* by a perception of a pinched nerve rather than *constituted* by it. Furthermore, perhaps calming your breathing mitigates anxiety not because when you do so you are no longer aware of rapid breathing, but because focusing on a gentle rhythm calms anxiety.

The subtraction argument

Although the research within the philosophy of mind regarding emotions relies on empirical data more than many other areas in philosophy of mind, James and contemporary defenders of body-based theories of emotions also lean on that old philosophical warhorse, the thought experiment, to support their view. The thought experiment they employ, the 'subtraction argument', asks us to imagine what is left of an emotion after we subtract the relevant bodily processes. For example, let's pretend that you are angry at your supervisor for having scheduled you to work over the winter holidays. Your co-worker is never asked to come into the office over the holidays because he has children to mind at home. You think this is patently unfair and it makes your blood boil. Now take away the heat and other relevant bodily sensations from this scenario. What's left? James argues that when we remove the awareness of bodily sensations, what's left is only a stark judgement of injustice that is bereft of emotional content. In James's words, 'if we fancy some strong emotion, and then try to abstract from our consciousness of it all the feelings of its characteristic bodily symptoms, we find we have nothing left behind, no "mind-stuff" out of which the emotion can be constituted, and that a cold and neutral state of intellectual perception is all that remains'.

James's subtraction argument applies equally well to other emotions. What would be left of your joy of taking a vacation if we were to anaesthetize the bodily feeling of elation? You would believe that you are extraordinarily happy. Yet this bare belief, proponents of body-based theories maintain, is not an emotion.

Problems for body-based theories

Critics of James's account sometimes point out that it fails to explain unconscious emotions. Although we have conscious emotions, it is generally thought that we also have feelings that lie below the surface, feelings that a psychiatrist or close friend might know we have even when we do not know it ourselves. Such emotions are capable of affecting our behaviour—for example, an unconscious fear of rejection might interfere with one's ability to enter a long-term romantic relationship—but they act on us behind the scenes. This is a problem for James. If an emotion is the awareness of a bodily change, then emotions are necessarily conscious. According to James, to fear rejection, is to consciously experience certain bodily changes—an elevated heart rate, bodily tension, and such like—caused by thoughts about long-term romantic commitments.

One might also wonder how a body-based account can explain the emotions of an actor who feels cheerful but is portraying sorrow. This would be a problem for the body-based account since the actor's body would take on a sorrowful bearing, and the actor would be aware of this bodily posture, yet not feel sad. There also seem to be emotions that do not have characteristic bodily states—guilt might be one such example—as well as differing emotions that have a common bodily manifestation—anger and fear both elevate the heart rate. Furthermore, emotions can exhibit intentionality (they can be about things): you may be happy that you completed a marathon, sad over the loss of a loved one, nostalgic about your childhood home. But it doesn't seem that bodily feelings are about such things, and, as we discussed in Chapter 4, may not even be about anything at all.

Defenders of body-based accounts of emotions have responses to these objections. Departing from a strictly Jamesian theory, Prinz, for example, argues that to experience an emotion is to perceive a bodily state, rather than to *feel* or be aware of a bodily state. Since perception need not be conscious, this allows for unconscious body-based emotions. Body-based theorists also have a broad view of what counts as a bodily change. Internal physiological changes count, and this could explain why the actor was happy though outwardly appearing sad. Body-based theorists also question whether, when this broader view of bodily changes is taken into account, there really are different emotions that have the same bodily signature. Finally, in accord with the causal account of intentionality, which we also discussed in Chapter 4, those who defend body-based accounts of emotion argue that bodily states acquire intentionality by being systematically connected to events in the world. Since seeing snakes systematically causes a soaring heart rate in humans, that elevated heart rate comes to represent fear.

One remaining objection is that emotions seem to have a normative component—they can be rational or irrational—and it is unclear how body-based theories can explain this. For example, if you were to scream in terror upon seeing Pineapple at your door, this would have been irrational; if you feel elated upon hearing good news, this is rational. But bodily states are neither rational nor irrational. Some body-based theorists have expanded their accounts to encompass appraisals while others have tried to squeeze normativity out of the causal relation between the emotions and what elicits them. Other philosophers take the normativity of emotions as reason to reject body-based views entirely.

Judgement-based theories of emotions

How else ought we to understand your fear upon hearing measured footsteps leading to your bedroom door? According to judgement-based theories of emotions, your fear in our opening imagined scenario comprises your judgement that an intruder was about to enter your room. Since judgements can be either rational or irrational, such views are designed to account for the normativity of emotions. They also are well suited to account for the intentionality of emotions. Judgements are clearly about things: you make judgements about intruders, about winning prizes, about family members. And judgements readily differentiate emotions such as anger and fear and can make sense of emotions that do not seem to have a characteristic bodily profile, such as guilt. Furthermore, such theories can easily account for the actor who dramatizes the feeling of grief yet feels happy and the paralytic who feels emotions. For these reasons, proponents of judgement-based theories see them as preferable to body-based accounts.

But what of James's subtraction argument? The philosopher Martha Nussbaum, who argues for a judgement-based account, wields her own subtraction argument. She asks us to consider grief. Although she admits that her feelings of grief typically coincide with certain bodily sensations and changes, she argues that if a doctor were to check her blood pressure and heart rate and found that the relevant bodily changes hadn't taken place, this would provide no reason to think that she was not grieving: 'if my hands and feet were cold or warm, sweaty or dry, again this would be of no critical value'. In other words, against the Jamesian subtraction argument, Nussbaum argues that we can take away all bodily sensations without taking away the emotion. What matters about an emotion, according to judgement-based accounts, is what is going on in your head rather than in your heart: emotions are the beliefs you have and judgements you make, not the awareness of your heart rate or other bodily processes.

Problems for the judgement-based account

The judgement-based account, though it has advantages, share of disadvantages too. For example, we generally think that some non-human animals feel emotions. Dogs, as any dog owner knows, are happy when their owners take them for walks and sad when left to fend for themselves. But are dogs making judgements? Infants have a range of emotions, but, if judgements require language and infants are pre-linguistic, it would seem that they do not make judgements.

Another problem for the judgement-based account is that we sometimes feel emotions that do not coincide with the judgement we are making. For example, I might judge that a roller coaster is perfectly safe yet feel fear when I ride it. If emotions are simply judgements, it would seem that if I judge the ride as safe, I should feel that it is safe. And emotions can be recalcitrant: after you learn that Pineapple was the intruder, you no longer judged the situation as threatening, yet your fear may have lingered. Body-based theorists also point out that often we make judgements without undergoing emotions at all. I might judge that crossing the street against the light is dangerous yet not feel afraid. Finally, by relegating bodily sensations and changes to mere accompaniments to emotions, judgement-based theories strike some as rather cold, more appropriate for a robot than a human being.

Judgement-based theorists have responses to these objections. Making a judgement does not require the use of language and when you judge that a roller coaster is safe yet feel afraid, you are making two contradictory judgements: one part of you is judging it's safe while the other part is judging it dangerous. And the same goes for recalcitrant emotions: after Pineapple entered, you assessed the situation as safe but also judged that you are still in danger. Finally, the relevant sense of judgement, the judgement-theorist will argue, is judgement in the full sense of incorporating belief. Fear is not only the judgement that a situation is dangerous, but it is the judgement along with the belief that it is dangerous. When beliefs are added to the equation, cases in which the mental side of the equation (the judgement and the belief) is present without the emotion, they claim, do not arise. And as to whether the judgement view is too cold to account for emotions, this is simply rejected: what it posits as emotions are no more cold and no less cold than emotions themselves.

Embodied emotions

Some philosophers maintain that mental processes are 'embodied', by which they mean that the body (in the sense, generally, of torso, limbs, head, neck, but not brain) is an integral part of our mental architecture, so much so that a disembodied mind makes no sense; thinking, perceiving, judging, experiencing are, at least to some extent, ways of moving your body. Taking their inspiration in part from the 20th-century French phenomenologist Maurice Merleau-Ponty, the embodiment theorists emphasize that it is with our bodies that we experience everything: 'the flesh is at the heart of the world' as Merleau-Ponty put it.

Might you be a bodyless brain, a brain housed in a vat of life-sustaining nutrients, connected via wires to a computer providing sensory input? And can't the experience of an amputee's phantom limb pain occur without the limb in question? Embodiment theorists maintain that a brain in a vat, if such a thing is possible, has emotions and other experiences only if it is sustained in a nutrient bath and given sensory input and that such externalities count as the brain's body. An amputee's phantom pain has a bodily manifestation as well, causing behavior in the remainder of the body. According to the Alva Noë, a contemporary American philosopher and proponent of the embodied mind theory, perceptual experience 'is not something that happens to us, or in us', but is rather 'something we do'.

The embodiment theorist's account of emotion resonates with James's and Lange's theories of emotion, yet also differs from them. James distinguishes the feeling of the bodily changes that result from a frightening sound, for example, from the bodily changes themselves, yet for the embodiment theorist, the dichotomy between mind and body is a false one. And while Lange sees emotions as bodily states that are controlled by the autonomic nervous system, which controls involuntary actions, such as heart rate and piloerection (goosebumps), embodiment theorists are more likely to connect emotions to the somatic nervous system, which controls voluntary actions such as reaching and walking.

The embodied account of emotions also has a behaviourist tinge. If you recall from Chapter 2, the behaviourist understands mental states as nothing more than certain types of bodily behaviour (as well as the disposition to behave in certain ways). And according to the embodiment theorist, all mental processes are distributed in your body, in the movements of your limbs or the furrowing of your brow, the clenching of a fist. 'The gesture', Merleau-Ponty says, 'does not *make me think* of anger; it is anger itself'. Yet, for the most part, the embodiment theorist does not aim to eliminate the first-person experience of consciousness.

For embodiment theorists, the body plays the leading if not exclusive role in the theatre of the mind. For example, some proponents of the embodied mind thesis understand athletes and dancers as thinking with their bodies and writers as, literally, thinking with their hands. And your body need not be of your own flesh and blood. For example, if you have prosthetic hands, once they are fully integrated into your actions, you could think with your prostheses. Embodiment theorists marshal phenomenology, or first-person insight, that suggests that amputees incorporate prostheses into their body image to support their view that thinking can extend to a prosthetic appendage.

Might you sometimes think with something that is not even part of your body, something of which you have no phenomenological experience at all? The next chapter addresses this question.

Chapter 7
Digital Minds

How many of your friends' phone numbers can you recite? Probably not many, or maybe none at all. In principle not spending time memorizing phone numbers should give us more time to think about things that really matter—graduating from medical school; getting married; your baby's first smile—yet in practice it's easier to take a photo.

Has our phone-enabled ease of acquiring information given rise to the contraction of human memory? Or should we think of our phones as memory-expanding devices, not merely mitigating our dwindling mental capacities but extending them, making us smarter, quicker, and better able to remember information?

Questions about the human–digital interface and the prospects of artificial intelligence are studied in philosophy of mind not only because they are intrinsically interesting—over the past fifty years, the number of transistors per chip has been doubling about every two years, and it is natural to wonder where this trend will lead—but also because of what they may reveal about the mind–body problem: if computers have thoughts, then physical devices can think and have understanding. Our brains might be one such physical device.

Where does your thinking occur?

When embroiled in thought, can you feel your brain working? After hours on end of tackling a difficult problem, you may say that your brain is tired, but do you experience that tiredness as being in your head? More generally, can introspection identify where our thinking takes place?

Whether there is a *phenomenology of thought*, is debated. Some philosophers argue that there is. Galen Strawson, for example, asks us to consider the difference between listening to a language you understand and one you don't. The two experiences, he argues, are phenomenologically distinct; they feel like different experiences; ergo, there is something it is like to understand each of them, and since understanding a language requires thought, there is something it is like to think. Others are not so sure, but in any case, even if there is something it is like to think, it does not follow that you have an experience of where your thinking takes place.

If introspective awareness were to provide direct insight into where thinking takes place, then even ancient cultures should have had a sense that thinking occurs in the brain. However, the brain has not always regarded as the emperor of thought. The Ancient Egyptians, for example, maintained that the heart was the locus of cognition, and they discarded the brain but preserved the heart during mummification, which, they believed, was weighed in the afterlife to determine whether the deceased would go to heaven (Figure 8). In Ancient Greece, Aristotle's heart-based, or 'cardiocentric', view of the mind was based on his work on animal dissection, which revealed that the heart was the origin of the veins of the body, while Plato's brain-based, or 'cephalocentric', view was inspired not by introspection, but by the work of the physician and anatomist Alcmaeon of Croton.

8. The Ancient Egyptian ibis-headed god of writing, Thoth, records the weighting of scribe Huefner's heart against the feather of Ma'at, which represents truth, justice, balance, and order. From the Book of the Dead, Papyrus of Ani, *c.*1250 BCE.

Although the heart-or-brain question has long been resolved in favour of the brain, philosophers who think that the mind extends to our digital devices do not see this as the end of the story. Yes, thinking occurs in our brains, such philosophers will say, but it is not limited to our brains; when our brains are coupled with our phones, it is the brain–phone system that does the thinking.

The extended mind

Imagine that Inga and Otto are both planning to visit the Museum of Modern Art. Inga has been there before. She reflects for a moment on where it is located, then heads towards West 53rd Street. Otto has visited the museum before as well. However, because he suffers from a peculiar form of amnesia that selectively targets his ability to form long-term brain-based memories of the location of buildings, Otto can't recollect locations in the way Inga can. However, his amnesia doesn't prevent him from going to the museum since he has a notebook, always near at hand, in which the addresses of all the places he likes to frequent are recorded. He consults it, pages over to 'M', holds the book open, and ends up meeting Inga in front of his favourite painting: Dalí's *The Persistence of Memory*. What should we say about Otto's memory of the museum's location? Does Otto fail to remember it? Or is Otto's memory of the location stored in his notebook?

This thought experiment is a variation of one that David Chalmers and Andy Clark devised to make a case for the view that our minds extend beyond the confines of our heads. Just as Inga remembers where the museum is because its location is engraved in her brain, Otto, as they see it, remembers where the museum is because its location is engraved in his notebook; just as Inga believed the museum was on West 53rd before consulting her memory—it is one of her many 'standing beliefs' (beliefs she has whether she is thinking about them or not)—Otto believed that the museum was on West 53rd before consulting his notebook because his notebook, when stored away, contains his standing beliefs about building locations. In all relevant respects, Chalmers and Clark argue, Otto's notebook functions like a brain-based memory: it's usually available when needed, easily and habitually relied on, and, in general, unreflectively accepted as true. When amputees depend on prosthetic limbs, we do not feel compelled to say that these limbs are not part of their bodies; a prosthetic leg becomes the amputee's leg. Similarly, according to Chalmers and Clark, Otto's notebook should count as a veritable part of his mind rather than a mere *aide-mémoire*.

Chalmers and Clark further defend their idea that the mind can extend beyond the confines of the skull by invoking what has been referred to as the 'parity principle'. According to this principle, a process in the external world counts as part of the mind if it is the case that the process would be a mental process, if it were to occur inside the head. In terms of Otto's notebook, the parity principle rules that its contents are part of his mind because if its contents were recorded inside his brain and the process of consulting them occurred internally (if, rather than opening the pages in the book and flipping to M for museums, he were to go through the alphabet in his mind), Otto would be consulting his memory. Otto and Inga go about accessing information about building locations differently, but, given that the contents of his notebook would count as part of the contents of Otto's mind if they were stored internally, the parity principle rules that when Otto consults his notebook, he is consulting his mind.

Should we accept the parity principle? Proponents acknowledge that there are significant dissimilarities between Otto's and Inga's beliefs about the museum's location. For example, Otto must carry out a few steps to access his notebook-based memory, whereas for Inga, the process is close to automatic. Otto could accidentally leave his notebook on the subway platform, whereas what is inscribed in Inga's brain always goes with her onto the train. But are such differences relevant to the question of whether Otto's mind extends to his notebook? Brain-based memories may also take some time to dredge up. We sometimes pause to reflect before recalling someone's name, and we can believe that the number of days in January is thirty-one even if we need to access this belief by going through the childhood ditty. And, while we don't leave them on subway platforms, we do sometimes lose our brain based memories.

Digital Minds

Another difference between brain-based memory and notebook-based memory is that brain-based memory is more labile, as it is often revised, while the information in Otto's notebook is static. But not only could Otto revise his notebook, it seems that if we were to have intransient memories, they would be memories all the same. Yet someone else could revise Otto's notebook without his consent. True, but we do not condone or explicitly allow entrance to everything that is stored in our brain-based memories either. An evil neurosurgeon who wants glowing reviews could covertly manipulate your brain, inserting the belief that a botched operation was a success. Indeed, one might even say that early childhood education is aimed at inserting beliefs into our heads whether we want them to be there or not.

How far does the mind extend according to the extended-minders? Thanks to an online New York City Department of Parks and Recreation map, you can access the species and location of every street tree in New York City. If the information from the map were stored in your head, we would probably say that you have an exceptional memory for NYC street trees. But as things stand, is it correct to say that you remember or at least know or have a standing belief that there is a pin oak on the corner of 22nd Street and Lexington Avenue? Why even stop at digital maps? The world is teeming with information. If I were to ask you, 'how many bridges are there in NYC?' you could bike around the five boroughs and count all 2,027 of them. If a representation of the city were stored in your head, and you were to imagine biking around counting up bridges, you would be relying on mental processes to come up with the answer. So does all of NYC count as part of your mind?

In addition to the question of how far the mind extends, one also wants to know when it extends. Chalmers and Clark's thought experiment concerns someone with a memory deficit, and perhaps we are more inclined to extend the minds of those who suffer from (brain-based) memory loss. We employ living wills, which specify one's preferences for medical and end of life care, should one no longer be able to express them. Perhaps in creating a living will, one uploads one's preferences onto a piece of paper. The issue is complicated, however, since ethicists disagree about whether living-will directives necessarily express one's preferences when one can no longer do so oneself. And then, what should we say about a final will and testament? Chalmers and Clark maintain that it is the 'coupled system' (the person plus the notebook) that houses the relevant beliefs. But could there be a sense in which one's desires persist within a will even after one suffers from that largest of memory deficits, death? Could the concept of the extended mind help us to, without depending on the idea of an immortal soul, make sense of our strong compunction to abide by a person's desires after they have died?

And what about consciousness? Does it extend beyond the skin? When you give someone power of attorney are your conscious decisions being created in someone else's brain? Or consider Janani, who is blind and uses a seeing-eye dog to help her navigate. If the processes that compose her seeing-eye dog's perceptual consciousness were to occur in Janini's brain, Janani would have visual conscious experiences. And as her dog is with her as reliably as Otto's notebook is with him, it seems that if Otto's beliefs extend onto his notebook, then Janani's consciousness extends into her dog; it seems that her conscious perceptual experience is in part housed in her seeing-eye dog's brain.

Should university exams be open phone?

The extended mind thesis has implications for education. If part of a person's mind can be stored externally, then in testing a student's knowledge, we should test the whole phone-and-brain-based student complex; to forbid the use of phones use would be an unjustified limitation, something like requiring you to take a heavy sedative before writing an exam.

The analogy, however, can be questioned. Perhaps banning the use of part of your internal mind on a test (by requiring you to take a sedative) is unreasonable since you benefit, all round, from learning and being tested when you are not sedated. But is it beneficial to always rely on your phone? It is true that for many jobs, one's Google IQ matters. But is it a good idea to offload memories en masse?

When a memory is stored on your cranial platform, in addition to being accessible, it has reverberating effects on your beliefs. For example, if Inga were to learn that the museum had been relocated to Castleton Corners on Staten Island, she would automatically revise her belief about the feasibility of a lunch break visit. But perhaps we can add the reverberations to the external system; technology more sophisticated than a notebook would be required, but automatic updates and reminders are now a way of life.

Your internally stored memories, however, also affect the way in which you learn new information and perceive and think about the world. When you memorize a poem, you are not only able to recite it but you may also perceive the world in terms of it. When Emily Dickinson's 'Autumn' is written down in a notebook, you can consult it when necessary but you won't see an autumn maple as wearing 'a gayer scarf'. Nor would storing Maya Angelou's 'Late October' on your phone rather than in your brain enable you to hear in the falling leaves the 'tinny sound of little dyings'. Images stored in the mind also affect us differently from images stored on our phones. After you see Monet's *San Giorgio Maggiore at Dusk* and incorporate it into your brain-based memory, sunsets might take on a new valence. Similarly, although consulting a digital bank of chess positions can let a player know that a position is an isolani (a queen's pawn with no like-coloured pawns on adjacent files), it doesn't enable the player to see it *as* an isolani. Learning one language, rather than using a translating program, can facilitate learning another, and learning basic mathematics facts, rather than relying on a calculator, may enable you to see patterns in more advanced mathematics. And while you may write down your parents' admonishments in a notebook, this form of stored information won't spark a feeling of guilt when you fail to call for your weekly chat.

Recent advocates of the external mind thesis tend to lean less on parity and more on the idea that external information becomes part of one's mind when it is available when needed, automatically relied on, and generally accepted as true. And technology more advanced than phones and notebooks, such as MIT Borglab's 'memory glasses', which are capable of providing wearers with subliminal memory prompts, may go some way towards bridging the gap between internal and external memories. But for now, there may be something to be said for closed book and closed phone examinations.

Do computers think?

Quite apart from the question of whether a phone's digital storage should count as an extension of the human mind is the question of whether phones and other computational devices have thoughts of their own. When computers make winning moves in chess, are they thinking about what moves to make? Do facial recognition programs that identify faces in a crowd have beliefs about what those faces looks like? Do chatbots understand what they are chatting about?

We often find it natural to speak as if computers think. Or at least, we find it natural to do so when they take some time to complete their tasks. But a question that torments philosophers is: do computers, regardless of what we are inclined to say about them, really think?

The 19th-century English mathematician Ada Lovelace argued that computers cannot manifest intelligence. Lovelace wrote one of the first computer programs and came up with the incipient idea of a 'universal computer' (which, like the computers of today, is one that can run arbitrary programs). Computers cannot think, she maintained, since they do only what we program them to do; a computer, in her words, 'has no pretensions whatever to *originate* anything [but can only] do *whatever we know how to order it* to perform'.

If a computer does only what it is programmed to do, does this mean it cannot think? When you perform a dance or recite a line of poetry just as you were taught, are you not thinking? This may be an interesting question to ponder, but we can puit aside since today we have self-teaching computer programs that are not fully constrained by our orders. For example, the computer program AlphaGo Zero taught itself to be the strongest Go player in the world in three days by playing against itself. AlphaGo Zero does more than what it was explicitly programmed to do, and even the best Go players in the world are mystified as to why it makes some of its moves.

The Ancient Mayan language room

Imagine that you are enclosed in a room and have been given the task of manually carrying out a computer program that responds to questions written in the Ancient Mayan language, a language that is a precursor to the Ch'orti' spoken today in eastern Guatemala and was actively used by many Mesoamerican people from about 200 to 300 BCE to the 16th-century Spanish Conquest. Ancient Mayan has an extremely elaborate script composed of roughly 800 symbols, or glyphs, some of which stand for syllables,

9. **Ancient Mayan glyphs in stone, from the ruins at Caracol, Belize.**

others for whole words and numbers (Figure 9). Inside this room, armed with a giant instruction manual that associates sets of Mayan glyphs that form questions with sets of Mayan glyphs that form answers to those questions, your job is to provide answers written in Mayan to questions given to you in Mayan. Nowhere in this manual are there explanations in English (or any other language you understand) of what any of the glyphs mean.

When a question comes in through a slot, you consult your rulebook, which associates shapes of a certain form (the questions) with shapes of another certain form (the answers), then meticulously write down the appropriate answer glyphs on a card and send it out through another slot. Even though your only exposure to the language is from the rulebook, you are able to provide answers to your questions that are indistinguishable from those that would have been given by the ancient scribes. It will be a painstaking task as the rulebook would be enormous. But let us assume it is in principle possible. The question is: 'Do you understand the Ancient Mayan language?'

Inside the room, you are, in essence, carrying out a computer program. The room is the hardware; the strings of symbols that arrive through the slot in the wall are the input; your rulebook is the program; the answers you produce are the output. And your job, as is a computer's, is merely to manipulate sets of symbols based on, not what they mean, but on a set of rules. Thus, if you don't understand the Mayan glyphs, it might seem that a computer designed to perform the same task wouldn't either. (Indeed, it might be argued that contemporary scholars studying Mayan glyphs are not in an entirely dissimilar position since although they can read every glyphic syllable, a full understanding of what the ancient carvers or scribes meant is, at least as of yet, elusive.)

The Mayan language room argument is a variation of a thought experiment devised by the contemporary American philosopher

John Searle, which, he maintains, illustrates that symbol-manipulating devices, such as today's digital computers, are incapable of understanding language; it illustrates that when you type questions into a chatbot, no matter how reasonable the answers may seem, the chatbot understands nothing of what you are saying.

Searle's thought experiment, published in 1980, generated great interest in both philosophy and artificial intelligence communities, and, though championed by some, has met with myriad objections, perhaps the most pressing of which is the 'system's reply'. This objection states that in responding to question-glyphs, you are merely the computer's central processing device; a central processing device does not understand language, but a computer as a whole does. Analogously, inside the room, you do not understand the glyphs, but the system as a whole, which includes the rulebook, does.

In response to this objection, Searle asks what would happen if you were to memorize the rulebook. You would then become the entire system, yet, according to Searle, you still would not understand the Ancient Mayan language. From your own point of view, you would only be associating one set of shapes with another set of shapes, only associating purely formal features of the symbols, without any understanding of what they mean. What this lack of understanding shows, according to Searle, is that 'syntax', which concerns the structure of language, 'is not sufficient for semantics', which concerns the meaning of language.

Is this correct? Is it impossible to squeeze meaning out of the meaningless zeros and ones that form the basis of computation? When you memorize the rulebook, your conscious mind, according to Searle, will still not glean the meaning of the glyphs. Would it matter if the relevant computer program were self-teaching? Would it matter, for example, if you were to have created the rulebook by searching the internet for questions in Ancient Mayan (pretending for the moment that there is a large community of people who regularly share online information in the language) and recording them in a database along with their answers? Doing so, according to Searle, would still not confer conscious understanding of classical Mayan.

But why? The debate over whether computers can understand language turns in part on whether consciousness is required for understanding. Searle sees understanding as a conscious process and thinks that silicon does not ground consciousness. However, others argue that because the task of carrying out a chatbot program is so enormous, we cannot know what it would be like to perform such a task, to say nothing of performing it at a processing speed of 3.8GHz, and thus cannot exclude the possibility that consciousness emerges from complex enough syntactic operations. Still others argue that the task of carrying out such a computer program is not even *in principle* humanly possible and, thus, that the thought experiment is unintelligible.

The Turing test

Alan Turing, the mathematician whose face is on Britain's £50 note in recognition of, among other things, developing the first fully-fledged theory of computability and playing a key role in cracking the German secret code during the Second World War, suggests that the question of whether a computer could think is too muddled to be addressed. He argues that we should instead ask whether a computer could make us believe it is thinking. And to clarify this question, he offers the following test: occlude both a computer and a human behind a screen and ask each of them questions; if we are unable to identify the source of the written responses (human or computer), then we would believe that the computer is thinking; the computer, as contemporary philosophers now say, would have passed the 'Turing test'.

Have any computers ever passed the Turing test? While there are computers that have fooled people for brief periods of time—people on dating sites, for example, have been duped for a while into thinking that a computer is the future love of their life—it is still fairly easy to trip a computer up. Or at least, it appears to be. Perhaps someone has secretly designed a program that has stood up to years of extended online correspondence, melting the hearts of thousands. Some philosophers, however, argue that not only has this never happened, but that it never could happen. As they see it, although our brains are finite, common sense is not since it allows us to make an indefinite number of judgements. You know, for example, that when you order kale juice at a juice bar, not only will the drink you receive be green—which any computer worth its silicon should also know—but also that it won't be served in an oil can, and that one of the recommended add-on options won't be butterscotch syrup. Such common sense is a prerequisite for successful communication, these philosophers argue, and thus no finite computer program will ever pass an extended, unrestricted Turing test. Others argue that although our common-sense knowledge is vast, it is not infinite and thus in principle programmable.

Most philosophy of mind discussions of the Turing test, however, do not concern the question of whether a computer could pass the test. Instead, parting company from Turing's original aim for the test, they concern whether passing the Turing test suffices for thought. The question here is only one of sufficiency. Passing the test is not a necessary condition for thought. A very intelligent, thinking computer (or human) might be classified as non-human, because it appears to know too much or think too quickly. Of course, such an intelligence might pass the test by dumbing itself down, yet it seems that one should not fail the test for performing too well. The concern, then, is whether passing the test suffices for intelligence.

Some philosophers argue that it obviously does not. A computer that follows the program we imagined you following in the Mayan room would pass the Turing test, yet, they argue, it would only be mechanically associating one string of sentences with another and would thus be no more intelligent than a toaster. Others think the answer is not so obvious. Any program that would pass the test would need to be enormous with lightning fast processing. And size and speed, they argue, matter. Moreover, if a computer were to exist that could pass the Turing test, we would, even after its identity is revealed, likely think of it as and refer to it as intelligent, and if we invariably did think of it as intelligent, the question of whether it actually is intelligent may, as Turing envisioned, become moot.

Those who argue that passing the Turing test does not suffice for intelligence can't see why size and speed should make a difference to whether we count something as a thinking thing. Children think of their stuffed animals as intelligent, they may point out, yet stuffed animals have no minds at all. As they see it, in attributing thought to a computer that passes the Turing test, we would be like a dog who, upon hearing a recorded bark, barks back thinking it is another dog. But the analogy may be faulty. The dog is thinking that the bark is coming from another dog; it's not, but the bark itself is a veritable bark. Similarly, we might think that a computer that passes the Turing test is human; it's not human, but the intelligence it manifests in doing so could be veritable intelligence.

Of course, as we touched on in Chapter 2, it is difficult to say what counts as intelligence, which makes it challenging to understand the very question, 'are computers intelligent?' Yet, since philosophy, as I suggested in the Preface, is perhaps more concerned with formulating questions than with finding answers, philosophers have tried to clarify what is at stake by reformulating the relevant question as: do computers have intelligence and minds in the same sense as human beings do? However, now it is not clear what 'the same sense' entails. Aeroplanes fly, but do they fly in the same sense as birds do? Do I have a mind in the same sense as Einstein has a mind? Do babies have minds in the same sense as adults? Does my cat have a mind in the same sense as I do? Would a genetically engineered genius have a mind in the same sense as a human whose mind developed in the ordinary way? If the point of studying artificial intelligence is to better understand the human mind, we must address the question of whether artificial minds are intelligent in the same way as humans are intelligent. However, if the point is to determine whether a mind—human or otherwise—can arise in a computer, the question of whether artificial minds are humanly intelligent can be ignored.

Where ethics and philosophy of mind intersect

Could there be computer consciousness? This question takes us back to the mind–body problem. For if computers are entirely physical objects, and if consciousness cannot arise in physical objects, then computers cannot be conscious. Is this a good argument? Until we have a solution to the mind–body problem, it is difficult to say. However, one can reject the idea of computer consciousness without rejecting the idea that physical systems can give rise to consciousness. Searle held both that consciousness could not arise in a digital computer, and that consciousness arises in physical systems; the brain, he thinks, is one such system. But what reason do we have to reject computer consciousness?

It is sometimes argued that if we allow for computer consciousness, it would be immoral to throw an old computer into the electronic waste bin, and that since it is not immoral to dispose of an old computer, computers are not conscious. However, if the day comes when we think of computers as conscious intelligent creatures, then two things are possible. On the one hand, we could revise our views about what type of treatment is morally required of us with respect to conscious creatures. Many people find it morally permissible to kill (presumably) conscious non-human animals so that we can enjoy eating them; maybe, when making moral evaluations, consciousness, per se, will not matter as much as our specific kind of consciousness or our specific kind of consciousness combined with our specific kind of intelligence. On the other hand, as in the past when we have realized the mistakes of our ways, we could revise our views about the moral permissibility of disposing of computers and keep our digital friends alive until they die of natural causes.

Computer intelligence poses a different moral quandary. If self-teaching and self-creating computers develop interests that are incompatible with human interests, our way of life could be threatened. Super-intelligent computers—computers capable of setting their own goals and with intelligence far surpassing human intelligence—might value wildlife and clean air over human life, which, as they see it, must be eradicated to prevent further global warming. Should we stop computers from developing interests that conflict with ours? Or would forcing a human point of view on another kind of intelligent creature be tantamount to imperialism? At its best, philosophy of mind can help us to address such questions, to think deeply about our place in the universe, and to understand—or if not to understand, then at least to question—what matters about being human.

References and further reading

Although interest may be the strongest indicator of how readable you'll find any of the following suggested books and articles, some assume more background knowledge than others, and few are very short. Use your judgement.

To further explore the depth and breadth of philosophy of mind, I recommend David Chalmers's anthology *Philosophy of Mind: Classical and Contemporary Readings* (Oxford University Press, second edition, 2021), which collects many of the works I refer to, as well as many to which I would have liked to refer had I not been trying to make this very short introduction very short. The same could be said of Maureen Eckert's collection *Theories of Mind: An Introductory Reader* (Rowman & Littlefield Publishers, 2006) and Brie Gertler and Lawrence Shapiro's *Arguing About the Mind* (Routledge, 2007). An anthology with an emphasis on the paradoxical nature of mind is Douglas Hofstadter and Daniel Dennett's *The Mind's I: Fantasies and Reflections on Self & Soul* (Basic Books, 2001). Hofstadter and Dennett's anthology was one of the books that sparked my interest in philosophy of mind when I read it as an undergraduate.

Preface

Some see debates over philosophical methodology as a waste of time; I enjoy them. If you do too, I recommend the introductory chapter of Bertrand Russell's *A History of Western Philosophy* (Routledge Classics, 1967) and Timothy Williamson's *Philosophical Method: A Very Short Introduction* (Oxford University Press, 2020).

As to the philosophical puzzles I begin with, Hyo-eun Kim, Nina Poth, Kevin Reuter, and Justin Sytsma scrutinize the experienced location of pain in 'Where is your pain? A Cross-Cultural Comparison of the Concept of Pain in Americans and South Koreans' in the February 2017 issue of *Studia Philosophica Estonica*; Martina Nida-Rümelin argues that some people do have inverted colour experiences in 'Pseudonormal Vision: An Actual Case of Qualia Inversion' (chapter 16 of Chalmers's anthology); and Isaac Asimov's *I Robot*—fiction that can also be understood as philosophy and is available through the Open Library, https://openlibrary.org/—probes computer intelligence, emotion, and consciousness, which are also topics of the last five references and recommendations associated with the final chapter of this book.

Chapter 1: Dualism

Frank Jackson presents his Mary-in-the-black-and-white-room argument in 'Epiphenomenal Qualia' (ch. 30 of Chalmers's anthology). Responses to it are legion, but a good starting point is David Lewis's 'What Experience Teaches', ch. 31 of Chalmers's anthology. And if you are interested in my response, please see B. Montero, 'Physicalism Could Be True Even if Mary Learns Something New', *Philosophical Quarterly*, 57 (2007), pp. 176–89.

The line of poetry about color, 'the Red—Blaze—is the Morning— | The Violet—is Noon—' is from Emily Dickinson's poem Poem 469.

Socrates' comment on how he understands death is from David Gallop's translation of Plato's *Phaedo* (Oxford University Press, 1975, rev. 2009).

The discussion of the interdependence of mind and body in the *Visuddhimagga*, translated by Ñāeamoli Bhikkhu, is freely available online, as is a text containing the hieroglyphics of the Egyptian *Book of the Dead* along with a transliteration, translation, and extended introduction by E. A. Wallis Budge (Dover Publications, 1985).

Wittgenstein's conception of philosophy as iatrogenic can be found in his book *Philosophical Investigations* (translated by G. E. M. Anscombe, Macmillan, 1968).

Aristotle presents his conception of nature in book II of the *Physics* (readily available online).

Descartes's argument for dualism is from the 'Sixth Meditation' of his *Meditations on a First Philosophy*. The entire text is freely available online and the 'Sixth Meditation' is ch. 1 of Chalmers's anthology. Jonathan Bennett's 2017 translation of the correspondence between Descartes and Princess Elisabeth is freely available online and the relevant letters are in Chalmers, ch. 3. And Noam Chomsky's take on the dissolution of Elisabeth's objection is presented in 'The Mysteries of Nature: How Deeply Hidden?', *The Journal of Philosophy*, 106, no. 4 (April 2009).

Leibniz argues for pre-established harmony in 'New System of Nature', which can be found in Leibniz's *Philosophical Essays*, edited and translated by R. Ariew and D. Garber (Hackett Publishing, 1989).

Berkeley's arguments for idealism can be found in the third of his *Three Dialogues between Hylas and Philonous in Opposition to Sceptics and Atheists* (available through Project Gutenberg) and is discussed by Keota Fields in his *Berkeley: Ideas, Immaterialism, and Objective Presence* (Lexington Books, 2011).

John Cottingham presents a case for understanding Descartes as a trialist in 'Cartesian Trialism', *Mind*, 94, no. 347 (1985), pp. 218–30, and Daniel Garber scrutinizes Descartes's trialistic response to Elisabeth in 'Understanding Interaction: What Descartes Should have Told Elisabeth', *The Southern Journal of Philosophy*, 21, no. S1 (1983).

K. Anthony Appiah argues for a trialistic understanding of the Akan conception of a person in 'Akan and Euro-American Concepts of Person', in Lee M. Brown (ed.), *African Philosophy: New and Traditional Perspectives* (Oxford University Press, 2004), pp. 21–34 and Kwame Gyekye for a dualistic conception in 'The Akan Concept of a Person' (Chalmers, ch. 4).

To read more about zombies, see Chalmers's book *The Conscious Mind* (Oxford University Press, rev. 1997) and his article 'Consciousness and its Place in Nature' (ch. 29 of his anthology). I criticize the idea that the possibility of zombies is inconsistent with physicalism in 'Must Physicalism Imply the Supervenience of the Mental on the Physical?', *The Journal of Philosophy*, 110, no. 2 (February 2013), pp. 93–110.

And don't miss the philosopher, logician, and magician, Raymond M. Smullyan's 'An Unfortunate Dualist' (Chalmers, ch. 7). The essay is from *5000 B.C. and Other Philosophical Fantasies* (St Martin's Press, 1984), which is another book—one of Smullyan's many—that sparked my interest in philosophy,

Chapter 2: Behaviourism

Gilbert Ryle presents his critique of dualism and his behaviouristic account of the mind in *The Concept of Mind*, available through the Internet Archive and excerpted in Chalmers's collection (ch. 8).

The psychologists J. B. Watson and B. F. Skinner lay out their behaviouristic theories in 'Psychology as the Behaviorist Views It', *Psychological Review*, 20 (1913), pp. 158–77, and *Science and Human Behavior* (The Free Press, 1965), respectively.

Hilary Putnam discusses the possibility of super-spartans, super-super-spartans, and their implications for behaviourism in *Brains and Behavior* (Cambridge University Press, 1975), ch. 10.

Wittgenstein offers his beetle-in-a-box thought experiment in *The Philosophical Investigations*, part I, sections 243–71.

A defence of behaviourism against the idea that it would imply that people can better know how you are feeling than you can is found in Paul Ziff's 'About Behaviourism', *Analysis*, 18 (1958), pp. 132–6.

Hegel argues for the behaviourist position that in determining intelligence, we must look at performance and not some inner light in the *Phenomenology of Spirit* (1807), trans. A. V. Miller (Oxford University Press, 1977), §322 and in *Logic: Being Part One of the Encyclopaedia of the Philosophical Sciences* (1830), trans. William Wallace (Oxford University Press, 1975), §140. And I discuss Hegel's conception of the mind in 'Philosophy of Mind in 19th Century Germany', in M. Forster and G. Kristen (eds), *The Oxford Handbook of 19th Century German Philosophy* (Oxford University Press, 2015), pp. 354–70.

The research on how valuing 'raw intelligence' may adversely affect hiring decisions is reported in S. J. Leslie, A. Cimpian, M. Meyer, and E. Freeland, 'Expectations of Brilliance Underlie Gender Distributions Across Academic Disciplines', *Science*, 347/6219 (2015), pp. 262–5.

Chapter 3: Physicalism

The question of just what the theory of physicalism amounts to is the focus of Jackson's 'Finding the Mind in the Natural World' (ch. 19) and my 'Post-Physicalism' (ch. 22); the question is also touched on in many of the other articles in sections C and D of Chalmers's anthology.

Laplace's conversation with Napoleon is described in Walter William Rouse Ball's *A History of the Study of Mathematics at Cambridge* (Cambridge University Press, 1889; reissued by the publisher, 2009).

J. J. C. Smart argues against behaviourism and for the mind–brain identity theory in 'Sensations and Brain Processes' (Chalmers, ch. 11).

The difficulty of identifying higher-level properties with lower-level ones is discussed by Noam Chomsky in 'Language and Nature', *Mind*, 104 (1995), pp. 1–61, Barbara Malt in 'Water is not H2O', *Cognitive Psychology*, 27 (1993), pp. 41–70, and Joseph Laporte in 'Living Water', *Mind*, 107, no. 426 (1998), pp. 451–5. These articles stand in opposition to both Saul Kripke's (1980) essentialist account of natural kinds, such as water and lightning, presented in *Naming and Necessity*, and Hilary Putnam's (1975) account of natural kinds in 'The Meaning of "Meaning"', excerpted in Chalmers, chs. 32 and 47, respectively. And if you want to delve into the nature of lightning, see Joseph R. Dwyer and Martin A. Uman, 'The Physics of Lightning', *Physics Reports*, 534, no. 4 (30 January 2014), pp. 147–242.

For a journey into cephalopod intelligence, see Peter Godfrey-Smith's 'On Being an Octopus' (Chalmers, ch. 65) as well as his *Other Minds: The Octopus, the Sea, and the Deep Origins of Consciousness* (Farrar, Straus and Giroux, 2016).

David Lewis likens functionalism to a detective story in 'Psychophysical and Theoretical Identifications', *Australasian Journal of Philosophy*, 50, no. 3 (1972).

Ned Block's argument against functionalism is presented in his 'Troubles with Functionalism', *Minnesota Studies in the Philosophy of Science*, 9 (1978), pp. 261–325 and excerpted in Chalmers, ch. 15.

Patricia Churchland discusses free will in 'The Big Questions: Do we Have Free Will?', NewScientist.com news service, 18 November 2006, and gives her take on the self in 'The Brain and its Self' (Chalmers, ch. 69), while David Hume's account of the self is presented in the section entitled 'Of Personal Identity' in his *Treatise of Human Nature* (readily available online). Of course, whether one counts Hume's conception of the self as revisionary depends on your starting point, for Hume's account of the self has some striking similarities to the Buddhist doctrine of *anatta*, according to which we possess no permanent underlying nature.

A discussion of the Buddhist concept of *anatta* can be found in ch. 6 of *What the Buddha Taught* by Walpola Rahula (1959).

Daniel Dennett probes the difficulty of differentiating a veritable sensory experience from an imagined one in his article 'Quining Qualia' (Chalmers, ch. 25). Further arguments for eliminativism can be found in Paul Churchland's 'Eliminative Materialism and the Propositional Attitudes' (Chalmers, ch. 45), and Valerie Hardcastle's *The Myth of Pain* (MIT Press, 1999).

David Papineau and I explain the causal argument for physicalism in 'Physicalism and Naturalism', in Kelly James Clark (ed.), *The Blackwell Companion to Naturalism* (2016) and in 'A Defense of the Via Negativa Argument for Physicalism', *Analysis*, 65, no. 3 (2005), pp. 233–7. For an extended explanation of my machine-switches metaphor, see my 'Varieties of Causal Closure', in H. D. Heckmann and S. Walter (eds), *Physicalism and Mental Causation* (Imprint Academic, 2003), pp. 173–87.

The idea that physics reveals only what things do and nothing of what things are is argued for by Bertrand Russell in *The Analysis of Matter* (Kegan Paul, 1927).

Panpsychist accounts of the mind are defended by Hedda Hassel Mørch in 'Is Matter Conscious', ch. 34 of Chalmers's anthology, and Galen Strawson in 'Realistic Monism: Why Physicalism Entails Panpsychism', *Journal of Consciousness Studies*, 13, nos. 10–11 (2006), pp. 3–31.

Arguments for non-reductive physicalism can be found in Jerry A. Fodor's 'Special Sciences' (Chalmers, ch. 18) and John Dupré's *The Disorder of Things: Metaphysical Foundations of the Disunity of Science* (Harvard University Press, 1995).

William Wimsatt offers an account of emergence that is consistent with reductionism in 'Emergence as Non-Aggregativity and the Biases of Reductionisms', *Foundations of Science*, 5 (2000), pp. 269–97. Wimsatt was my supervisor at the University of Chicago, where he helped me to understand that when philosophers simplify science, they risk missing crucially important insights. His *Re-Engineering Philosophy for Limited Beings: Piecewise Approximations to Reality* (Harvard University Press, 2007) makes a case for taking science at its word. Jessica Wilson presents a view that sits between non-reductive physicalism and dualism in *Metaphysical Emergence* (Oxford University Press, 2021). And Philip Anderson's classic paper 'More is Different' published in *Science* in 1972, is readily available online.

Chapter 4: Intentionality

Hilary Putnam discusses intentionality, including a variation on the question of whether debris washed up by the surf could count as a picture of something, in 'Brain in a Vat', which is ch. 1 of his *Reason, Truth and History* (Cambridge University Press, 1981).

Franz Brentano presents his views of object-directedness in 'Mental and Physical Phenomena', excerpted in Chalmers's anthology (ch. 35).

Elizabeth Anscombe's account of intentionality including her distinction between what has since been called 'mind-to-world direction of fit' and 'world-to-mind direction of fit' can be found in her book *Intention* (Basil Blackwell, second edition 1963). John Searle, in his *Intentionality* (Cambridge University Press, 1983), further analyses this distinction and contrasts intrinsic from derived—or what he refers to as 'observer relative'—intentionality.

The puzzles of intentionality that I mention are discussed in ch. 2 of Michael Thau's *Consciousness and Cognition* (Oxford University Press, 2002). A.J. Ayer offers his solution to the problem of how perceptions of windows and hallucinations of windows can seem to be about the same thing in 'The Argument from Illusion' (excerpted in Chalmers, ch. 52). And for an in-depth exploration of how to think about objects that do not exist, see Tim Crane's *The Objects of Thought* (Oxford University Press, 2013).

Edmund Husserl argues that consciousness is always consciousness of an object in 'The Paris Lectures', which can be found in *Phenomenology and Existentialism*, edited by Robert C. Solomon (Littlefield Adams Quality Paperbacks, 1980), pp. 43–57.

Jerry Fodor remarks that intentionality 'must be really something else' on p. 97 of his *Psychosemantics* (MIT Press, 1987).

Locke presents his view that ideas—specifically ideas of what he refers to as 'primary qualities'—resemble what they are ideas of in book II of *An Essay Concerning Human Understanding* (readily available online), and Nelson Goodman criticizes the resemblance account of representation in *Languages of Art: An Approach to a Theory of Symbols* (Hackett Publishing Company, second edition 1976).

Wittgenstein's discussion of the ambiguity of pictures is in part 1 of his *Philosophical Investigations*.

Attempts to naturalize intentionality can be found in Fred Dretske's 'A Recipe for Thought' and Ruth Millikan's 'Biosemantics', and a criticism of the naturalizing approach can be found in Kathleen

Akins's 'Of Sensory Systems and the "Aboutness" of Mental States' (chs. 37, 39, 38, respectively, of Chalmers's anthology).

The connection between intentionality and conscious experience is explored by Terence Horgan and John M. Tienson in 'The Intentionality of Phenomenology and the Phenomenology of Intentionality' (Chalmers, ch. 41).

Chapter 5: Consciousness

William James writes of our certainty that consciousness exists in part VI of *The Will to Believe*, available through Project Gutenberg.

In 'Troubles with Functionalism' (excerpted in Chalmers, ch. 15), Ned Block applies the Louis Armstrong quip about jazz to consciousness.

In *Mind, Language and Society* (Weidenfeld & Nicolson, 1999), John Searle defines consciousness as 'those states of sentience or awareness that typically begin when we wake up in the morning from a dreamless sleep and continue throughout the day until we fall asleep again'.

Thomas Nagel, 'What Is It Like to Be a Bat?' (Chalmers, ch. 24), argues that to be conscious is for there to be 'something it is like to be you'. L. A. Paul unfolds the concept of 'transformative experience' in *Transformative Experience* (Oxford University Press, 2015) and in What You Can't Expect When You're Expecting (Chalmers, ch. 6). And I discuss the sense in which we do not even know what it is like to be ourselves in 'What Experience Doesn't Teach: Pain Amnesia and a New Paradigm for Memory Research', *Journal of Consciousness Studies*, 27 (2020).

David Rosenthal distinguishes creature consciousness from state consciousness in 'Explaining Consciousness' (Chalmers, ch. 26).

Fred Dretske distinguishes thing-consciousness from fact-consciousness in 'Conscious Experience', *Mind*, 102/406 (1993), pp. 263–83.

The distinction between phenomenal consciousness and access consciousness is the focus of Ned Block's article 'On a Confusion about a Function of Consciousness', which was published along with commentaries by twenty-eight scholars in *Behavioral and Brain Sciences*, 18 (1995), pp. 227–47; an abridged and revised version of Block's article can be found in Chalmers's anthology, ch. 23.

In 'Skill and Consciousness', in Ellen Fridland and Carlotta Pavese (eds), *The Routledge Handbook of Philosophy of Skill and Expertise* (2020), I discuss the role of conscious attention in skill and argue, among other things, that current scientific data on the time it takes to be conscious of a stimulus does not preclude the possibility that tennis players consciously think before they strike.

As for scientific investigations into consciousness, the psychologist Bernard J. Baars puts forth his global workshop theory of consciousness in *A Cognitive Theory of Consciousness* (Cambridge University Press, 1988), the neuroscientist and psychiatrist Giulio Tononi lays out his theory of consciousness in 'An Information Integration Theory of Consciousness', *BMC Neuroscience*, 5 (2004), and Francis Crick and Christof Koch present their proposal for the neural correlates of consciousness in 'Towards a Neurobiological Theory of Consciousness', *Seminars in the Neurosciences*, 2 (1990), pp. 263–75.

David Chalmers presents his conception of 'the hard problem' in his article 'Facing Up to the Problem of Consciousness', *Journal of Consciousness Studies*, 2 (1995), pp. 200–19.

The idea that consciousness is without a function is broached by David Rosenthal in his paper 'Consciousness and its Function', *Neuropsychologia*, 48 (2008), pp. 829–40 and by Jaegwon Kim in his causal exclusion argument, presented in his 2000 book *Mind in a Physical World*, excerpted in Chalmers's anthology, ch. 20. Karen Bennett in her 'Why the Exclusion Problem Seems Intractable and How, Just Maybe, to Tract it', *Noûs*, 37 (2003), pp. 471–97, illustrates a possible way around Kim's arguments, and in *Thought in Action: Expertise and the Conscious Mind* (Oxford University Press, 2016), I explore the role of conscious attention in expert action; see the final chapter for a more extended discussion of the analogy between peripheral thought and peripheral vision.

Chapter 6: Emotions

Jesse Prinz identifies what he refers to as 'the problem of parts' and presents his Jamesian account of emotions in his *Gut Reactions: A Perceptual Theory of Emotion* (Oxford University Press, 2004). William James's own account of emotions, including his subtraction argument, is presented in his article 'What is an Emotion', published in the journal *Mind*, 9 (1884), pp. 188–205, and freely available online, as is Carl Lange's kindred view, which he expresses in his 1885 book *The Mechanism of the Emotions*, translated from the Danish by Benjamin Rand.

The study suggesting that taking acetaminophen can alleviate emotional pain is C. N. Dewall, G. Macdonald, G. D. Webster,

C. L. Masten, R. F. Baumeister, C. Powell, et al., 'Acetaminophen Reduces Social Pain: Behavioural and Neural Evidence', *Psychological Science*, 21, no. 7 (2010), pp. 931–7, doi: 10.1177/0956797610374741 PMID: 20548058.

Jonathan Cole's book *Still Lives* (MIT Press, 2006) explores, among other things, the emotional lives of people with spinal cord injuries that have left them to a large degree without sensation in their bodies.

Recalcitrant emotions—specifically their role in social and political contexts—are considered by Susan James in "Passion and Politics," published in *Philosophy and the Emotions edited by Anthony Hatzimoysis* (Cambridge University Press, 2010).

R. C. Solomon (ed.), *Thinking about Feeling: Contemporary Philosophers on Emotions* (Oxford University Press, 2004) contains Martha Nussbaum's argument for a judgement-based theory of emotions, which she presents in 'Emotions as Judgements of Value and Importance', pp. 183–99.

Maurice Merleau-Ponty claims that 'the flesh is at the heart of the world' in *The Visible and the Invisible*, trans. Alphonso Lingis (Northwestern University Press, 1968) and identifies a threatening gesture with the anger itself in *Sense and Nonsense*, trans. Hubert L. Dreyfus and Patricia Allen Dreyfus (Northwestern University Press, 1964).

Shaun Gallagher and Dan Zahavi explore the embodied account of the mind in 'The Embodied Mind' (Chalmers, ch. 51). An embodied account of the emotions, specifically, can be found in Giovanna Colombetti and Evan Thompson, 'The Feeling Body: Toward an Enactive Approach to Emotion', in W. F. Overton, U. Müller, and J. Newman (eds), *Body in Mind, Mind in Body: Developmental Perspectives on Embodiment and Consciousness* (Lawrence Erlbaum, 2006) and in Colombetti's *The Feeling Body: Affective Science Meets the Enactive Mind* (MIT Press, 2017). Alva Noë's conception of perceptual experience as something we do rather than something that happens to us is developed in his *Action in Perception* (MIT Press, 2006).

Chapter 7: Extended and digital minds

Galen Strawson considers the phenomenal feel of thinking in his article 'Cognitive Phenomenology: Real Life', in T. Bayne and

M. Montague (eds), *Cognitive Phenomenology* (Oxford University Press, 2011).

Andy Clark and David Chalmers argue that the mind extends beyond the boundaries of the skin in 'The Extended Mind' and Brie Gertler presents a criticism of their view in 'Overextending the Mind?' (chs 49 and 50 of Chalmers's anthology).

Wittgenstein probes the phenomenon of 'seeing-as' in his *Philosophical Investigations*, Part II (renamed Philosophy of Psychology—A Fragment in the Blackwell 2009 edition). Susanna Siegel discusses various senses of 'seeing-as' in *The Contents of Visual Experience* (Oxford University Press, 2010). And in future work I hope to develop my ideas on the way in which internally stored memories shape perceptual experience.

Ada Lovelace's argument against the idea of computer intelligence as well as her theory of a universal computing machine can be found in her article 'Translator's Notes to an Article on Babbage's Analytical Engine', in *Scientific Memoirs*, ed. R. Taylor, vol. 3 (1842), pp. 691–731.

The Mayan room thought experiment is a variation of an argument presented by John Searle in *Minds, Brains, and Programs* (ch. 76 of Chalmers's anthology). John Bodel and Stephen Houston (ed.), *The Hidden Language of Graphic Signs* (Cambridge University Press, 2021) gives you a sense of the challenges translators face when trying to understand the larger interpretative contexts of intricate systems of writing.

Alan Turing presents his views on artificial intelligence in 'Computing Machinery and Intelligence', which is excerpted in Chalmers's anthology, ch. 75.

The possibly Sisyphean task of hard-coding common-sense rules undertaken by Cycorp is discussed here: <http://www.alanturing.net/turing_archive/pages/Reference%20Articles/what_is_AI/What%20is%20AI08.html>.

And don't miss Terry Bisson's 'They're Made of Meat' (Chalmers, ch. 74).

Index

For the benefit of digital users, indexed terms that span two pages (e.g., 52–53) may, on occasion, appear on only one of those pages.

THE MEANING OF LIFE

A Very Short Introduction

Terry Eagleton

'Philosophers have an infuriating habit of analysing questions rather than answering them', writes Terry Eagleton, who, in these pages, asks the most important question any of us ever ask, and attempts to answer it. So what is the meaning of life? In this witty, spirited, and stimulating inquiry, Eagleton shows how centuries of thinkers - from Shakespeare and Schopenhauer to Marx, Sartre and Beckett - have tackled the question. Refusing to settle for the bland and boring, Eagleton reveals with a mixture of humour and intellectual rigour how the question has become particularly problematic in modern times. Instead of addressing it head-on, we take refuge from the feelings of 'meaninglessness' in our lives by filling them with a multitude of different things: from football and sex, to New Age religions and fundamentalism.

'Light hearted but never flippant.'

The Guardian.

INFORMATION
A Very Short Introduction
Luciano Floridi

Luciano Floridi, a philosopher of information, cuts across many subjects, from a brief look at the mathematical roots of information - its definition and measurement in 'bits'- to its role in genetics (we are information), and its social meaning and value. He ends by considering the ethics of information, including issues of ownership, privacy, and accessibility; copyright and open source. For those unfamiliar with its precise meaning and wide applicability as a philosophical concept, 'information' may seem a bland or mundane topic. Those who have studied some science or philosophy or sociology will already be aware of its centrality and richness. But for all readers, whether from the humanities or sciences, Floridi gives a fascinating and inspirational introduction to this most fundamental of ideas.

'Splendidly pellucid.'

Steven Poole, The Guardian

RISK
A Very Short Introduction
Baruch Fischhoff & John Kadvany

Risks are everywhere. They come from many sources, including crime, diseases, accidents, terror, climate change, finance, and intimacy. They arise from our own acts and they are imposed on us. In this *Very Short Introduction* Fischhoff and Kadvany draw on both the sciences and humanities to show what all risks have in common. Do we care about losing money, health, reputation, or peace of mind? How much do we care about things happening now or in the future? To ourselves or to others? All risks require thinking hard about what matters to us before we make decisions about them based on past experience, scientific knowledge, and future uncertainties.

www.oup.com/vsi